P9-DIG-016

Till Armageddon

Other books by Billy Graham

Angels: God's Secret Agents
Billy Graham Talks to Teen-agers
The Challenge: Sermons from Madison Square Garden
World Aflame
My Answer
The Secret of Happiness: Jesus' Teaching on Happiness As
  Expressed in the Beatitudes
Peace with God
The Jesus Generation
How to Be Born Again
The Holy Spirit

Billy Graham

Till Armageddon

A Perspective on Suffering

WORD BOOKS
PUBLISHER
WACO, TEXAS

TILL ARMAGEDDON: A PERSPECTIVE ON SUFFERING

Copyright © 1981 by Billy Graham

All rights reserved. No portion of this book may be reproduced in any form whatsoever, except for brief quotations in reviews, without written permission from the publisher.

Unless otherwise indicated, Scripture quotations are from the New International Version of the Bible, published by The Zondervan Corporation, copyright © 1978 by New York Bible Society International, and are used by permission.

Quotations from the New Testament marked AMPLIFIED are from the *Amplified New Testament,* © The Lockman Foundation 1954, 1958. Used by permission.

Quotations from the Old Testament marked AMPLIFIED are from *The Amplified Bible, Old Testament,* copyright © 1962, 1964 by Zondervan Publishing House. Used by permission.

Quotations marked PHILLIPS are from *The New Testament in Modern English* by J. B. Phillips, published by The Macmillan Company, © 1958, 1960, 1972 by J. B. Phillips, and are used by permission of the publisher.

Quotations marked ASV are from the American Standard Version, 1901, published by Thomas Nelson & Sons.

Quotations marked KJV are from the Authorized or King James Version of the Bible.

ISBN 0-8499-0195-2
Library of Congress Catalog Card Number 80-51485
Printed in the United States of America

First printing, February 1981
Second printing, March 1981

Contents

God could have kept Daniel out of the lion's den. . . . But God has never promised to keep us out of hard places. . . . What He has promised is to go with us through every hard place, and bring us through victoriously.

MERV ROSELL

Preface

ONE OF the oldest books in the world states, "Man is born to trouble as surely as sparks fly upward" (Job 5:7).

Never have these words been truer than today.

The whole world is sighing and suffering on a scale perhaps not known in human history: the refugees, the starving, the "new slaves," the psychological woes, the emotional turmoils, the broken marriages, the rebellious children, the terrorism, the hostages, the wars, and a thousand other troubles which beset every country in the world. There are no people anywhere that are immune. The rich and famous suffer as well as the poor and obscure. As the late actor Peter Sellers said, "Behind the mask of all us clowns is sadness and broken hearts."

It seems that the human race may well be heading toward the climax of the tears, hurts, and wounds of the centuries— Armageddon!

Suffering is the common lot of all people everywhere— believers and non-believers alike. But Christians often have their own particular types of sufferings in addition to the normal range of human miseries. Many times they suffer because they are followers of Jesus Christ. And many times they cry out with the psalmist, "Has God forgotten to be merciful? Has he in anger withheld his compassion?" (Ps. 77:9).

It is an ancient cry—echoed today by millions of people around the world. Why is there evil? Where did it all start, and why does God allow the terrible nightmare of suffering and evil to continue in human history? Why do the prayers for the overthrow of wickedness and for the victory of justice and righteousness seemingly go unanswered? And why are Christians not exempt from suffering—including persecution?

These are not easy questions to answer, and in reality we will never know the answer completely until we see our Lord face to face in heaven. Nevertheless, the Bible does give us some answers, and in this book I have tried to see what clues the Bible offers us to this universal question—the question of suffering.

But this study of the subject of suffering is not an academic or intellectual exercise, attempting to answer abstract philosophical questions which are unrelated to everyday living. No, as we shall see in these pages, even if we may not always understand why God allows certain things to happen to us, we *can* know He is able to bring good out of evil, and triumph out of suffering.

And so my concern in writing this book has been practical— to see what the Bible teaches us about suffering: how we should view it, and how we should prepare for it. What if you had just been notified you had six months to live because of incurable cancer? Or what if a loved one were suddenly stricken by a massive heart attack or critically injured in an automobile accident? What if you were taken hostage or cast into prison because of your faith in Christ? Or what about a thousand and one other personal crises—big and small—which could press upon us (or may already be pressing upon you right now)? How should you prepare for tragedy, or sorrow, or suffering, whatever its nature or source may be? How can you prepare *now* for the personal armageddons of the future— the battles we all face which threaten to overwhelm us? And how can you prepare for the great future Armageddon, which will mark the climax of world suffering and the ultimate overthrow of evil?

In *Till Armageddon* I try to deal with these and similar

questions—questions I believe to be of critical importance for each one of us.

Mount Everest was never climbed in a day. Those who attempt to climb its treacherous slopes spend months, even years, in training and in practice. Each small mountain conquered prepares one for a higher mountain and a tougher climb ahead.

So, too, the best preparation for tough times ahead are the little daily difficulties and how we react to them.

But my concern has also been to show another dimension of the Bible's teaching about suffering—the dimension of hope. Some day all the pain and suffering of this world will be gloriously banished. Because of what Jesus Christ did for us through His cross and Resurrection, we know that we have hope for the future. We know that in heaven every sin and evil will be banished, and suffering will be no more. The apostle Paul said, "I consider that our present sufferings are not worth comparing with the glory that will be revealed in us. The creation waits in eager expectation for the sons of God to be revealed. For the creation was subjected to frustration, not by its own choice, but by the will of the one who subjected it, in hope that the creation itself will be liberated from its bondage to decay and brought into the glorious freedom of the children of God" (Rom. 8:18–21).

In *Till Armageddon* I attempt to show something of what the future life is going to be like. In so doing we are going to see how the glory which lies ahead is far greater than any sufferings we might endure here.

But in the meantime—*Till Armageddon*—you and I are called to learn what it means to trust God in every circumstance, and to live for Him no matter what comes our way. My prayer is that God will use this book to help us think more clearly about suffering, and to rearrange our priorities so that when Armageddon comes—or our personal armageddons come—we will not be taken by surprise or be unprepared. Like Joseph storing up grain during the years of plenty to be used during the years of famine that lay ahead, may we store up the truths of God's Word in our hearts as much as possible, so that we are prepared for whatever suffering we are called upon to endure.

As an army officer once said, "Weather in war is always favorable if you know how to use it."

May this book help us to learn how to "use the weather," whatever it may be.

I have written this book, I must admit, with much reluctance. There are many, many others who have been through fires of suffering much more severe than those I have known, and as a result, they have experienced the grace and strength of God in far deeper measure. And yet God has been teaching me much about this subject—through personal experience, through the lives of others, and supremely through the Bible, His Word. I pray that through this book God will bring hope and encouragement to you—and challenge as well—as He has brought these to me during the writing of it.

Many times in the midst of the troubles and difficulties of my own life two little words have stood out, "Fear Not." I have often called those two little words the divine hush for God's children. But I have found that faith must lay hold of Christ, and we must live in godly fear. As the little child when hushed to sleep nestles on the mother's bosom, God's children need the calming, the "fear not" of the Scriptures in these days of fear and trembling. He still speaks to us as He spoke to Abraham, "Do not be afraid . . . I am your shield, your very great reward" (Gen. 15:1); and to Joshua, "Do not be afraid; do not be discouraged" (Josh. 8:1); or, "Peace! Do not be afraid. You are not going to die" (Judg. 6:23); "Don't be afraid, . . . Those who are with us are more than those who are with them" (2 Kings 6:16); "I will fear no evil, for you are with me" (Ps. 23:4); "The Lord is my light and my salvation—whom shall I fear?" (Ps. 27:1); "Why should I fear when evil days come . . . ?" (Ps. 49:5); "The Lord is with me; I will not be afraid. What can man do to me?" (Ps. 118:6); "Do not fear, for I am with you" (Isa. 41:10); "Do not be afraid, little flock, for your Father has been pleased to give you the kingdom" (Luke 12:32); "Do not be afraid. I am the First and the Last. I am the Living One; I was dead, and behold I am alive for ever and ever! And I hold the keys of death and Hades" (Rev. 1:17,18).

I have found the older I get that God never forgets anything. He knows all things, and He remembers His people, their sorrows, their sufferings, and all their needs. The only thing He forgets is our sins. "I, even I, am he who blots out your transgressions, for my own sake, and remembers your sins no more" (Isa. 43:25).

Nothing can touch the child of God without God's permission. So we accept each hurt, each problem, each difficulty as from His hand, seeking to learn from it all that He would teach us—using all the resources of God at our disposal and asking Him to make it turn out for our good and His glory.

Naturally, I have not done all the work on this book alone. Without the help of a number of people it would have been impossible. In the two years I spent (off and on) writing this book, I had the constant help of my wife, Ruth; my secretary, Stephanie Wills; my associate, John Akers; Elsie Brookshire, Lucille Lytle and the others in my Montreat office. In addition, I want to thank those who read the manuscript and made many helpful suggestions: my longtime friend Carole Carlson; Canon Frank Colquhoun of the Anglican Church in England; Millie Dienert, our longtime friend and companion on holidays (along with her husband); my associate in the Minneapolis office, Ralph Williams; Estelle Brousseau of Montreat-Anderson College; and Al Bryant of Word, Incorporated.

In studying and writing on this subject my own life has been deepened, and I have rededicated my life to helping those who are hurting spiritually, physically, and psychologically. It is my prayer that this book will not only help and inspire many suffering Christians, but will be used of God to bring many non-believers to a saving knowledge of Jesus Christ.

BILLY GRAHAM
September 15, 1980
Montreat, North Carolina

Till Armageddon

Then they gathered the kings together to the place that in Hebrew is called Armageddon.

REVELATION 16:16

1/

The Coming Storm

MANY WRITERS are predicting that the headlines of the eighties will continue to scream: war, violence, assassinations, torture, World War III—the real war, Armageddon.

There is no doubt that global events are preparing the way for the final war of history—the great Armageddon! As the earthly time clock ticks off each second and the world approaches midnight, this planet, according to the Bible, is going to be plunged into suffering too horrible to imagine or comprehend. As the top of Mount St. Helens blew off early in 1980 and became one of the great disasters of that period, so the Bible teaches in Hebrews 12 that God is going to shake the whole earth. The Bible says, "Once more I will shake not only the earth but also the heavens" (Heb. 12:26). The tremors that are leading to the greatest earthquake of all time are now being felt throughout the world.

Holocaust in the Wings

The ancient prophets warned about a time toward the end of history when people would be saying "'Peace, peace,' . . . when there is no peace" (Jer. 6:14). Thousands of peace conferences have been held since World War II, and yet the headlines continue to shout about war, violence, death and streaming refugees. Governments of the world are rocked with assassinations and bloodshed.

Yet only a few years ago it was fashionable to write or suggest that the world was entering a great era of peace. We were told by many idealists that utopia would be ushered onto the scene, along with all the technological miracles of our time. The dream was an illusion. We should have learned from history. They dreamed of peace in the earlier part of the century, but that was shattered by World War I. They dreamed and planned for peace after World War I, but World War I was only a preparation for World War II. Now the signs are everywhere that the world is preparing feverishly for World War III, which could be the last war—Armageddon!

Permeating the media is the concentration on catastrophic titles. Our movie theaters are jammed with the crowds who thrive on the disaster movies. The list of titles in any major city, like London, New York or Los Angeles, is almost endless with titles suggesting the most fearsome, unreal—and sometimes real—fantasies.

Even the most cheerful optimists are predicting the probabilities of an increase in suffering in our wounded world. One of the most cheery programs on television is ABC's "Good Morning America." But sometime ago Rona Barrett was interviewing someone from the CIA who reported that germs capable of destroying nations have already been developed. There are new viruses, he said, that could cause a breakdown in the health of the populace of an entire continent. Chemical and germ warfare are part of the arms arsenal now being developed throughout the world. Articles and documentary films are constantly being released, reporting that before the end of the century insects could be in control of our planet. One major newspaper concluded an editorial with the words: "There is a feeling that one is seeing the world in its twilight."

Expressions like "racial suicide," "racial genocide," "the end of the world" and "the end of the human race" are cropping up in conversations, journals and motion pictures throughout the world.

Terrorist groups are growing more and more daring in their attacks on others. Almost daily reports of new atrocities fill our newspapers. The president of a West African government was killed, his son beheaded, and many members of his staff executed publicly by a firing squad. The story was a comparatively insignificant item buried in the back pages of the violence-filled daily newspaper that I read.

Nuclear weapons, germ warfare, and precarious international relationships are not the only indications of civilization on a collision course. Our scientists are warning us that great climatic changes are in store for our world. We are told that the polar icecap seems to be slightly shifting, and this could affect our food-growing capabilities. Feeding the growing world population is an increasing burden.

The statistics on the increase in earthquakes almost break the computer.

On the moral front, things look extremely bleak, especially through Judeo-Christian eyes. There is something of an explosion in the breakdown of marriages and the almost total rejection of moral law and guidelines. Drugs and alcohol are destroying the minds of millions. The emergence of satanic cults and witchcraft is especially widespread in America and Europe.

Pleasure has become the goal of millions. Hedonism is now almost in control. Pornography meets with little restraint. A publisher told me at Oxford that over 80 percent of modern novels center in perversion and the flouting of the moral law.

On every hand people are screaming for "liberation" and social justice. It seems the rich are getting richer and the poor are getting poorer. This is true of nations as well as individuals. The economic strength of the world has shifted to the oil-producing countries who have amassed billions they do not know how to spend. While Western Europe and America go deeper in debt, the Third World lives on the knife-edge of starvation.

The theory that the world is getting better and better, and solving its political, economic and social problems, is no longer taught with very much confidence. We are living in a day of serious turmoil and trouble, and most thinking people to whom I talk forecast that things are going to get worse instead of better.

The Root of the Problem

Today we see a world which is unparalleled in its unrest, whether it is the unrest of the individual human heart, or of the social, political, or even religious, situation. The world is in the confusion and mess it's in today because it has rejected God and His moral order. The Scriptures themselves make it clear that when God's law is discarded, the only intelligent, unifying principles for human life and conduct are also cast away.

With this rebellion against God, mankind has lost its sense of purpose and meaning in life and denied the worth of human personality, and the other values that make life worthwhile. Most people of the world have some belief in a supernatural being—but we act like atheists! We think like atheists! We live and plan as if there were no God. We are living in a world that does not recognize God. When everyone does what is right in his own eyes, there is no possibility of order and peace. There will be more and more confusion and turmoil as people follow their own wicked devices.

Man is a rebel, and a rebel is naturally in confusion. He is in conflict with every other rebel. For a rebel by his very nature is selfish. He is seeking his own good and not the good of others. Sometimes through rationalization there can emerge unbiblical goals that seem for a time to have a unifying effect upon man, even creating mob interest and unity for a time—but these goals are temporary. There is no depth or meaning to them, and therefore these elements cannot bring unity to society.

The Bible indicates that in rejecting God and His principles for governing life, the world is heading for a situation of tension, confusion and turmoil that will ultimately set the stage for a future evil world ruler or system—the Antichrist.

The Antichrist and Armageddon

While God has a plan for man's good, the devil also has a master plan. He will bring to power a counterfeit world ruler or system that will establish a false utopia for an extremely short time. The economic and political problems of the world will *seem* to be solved. But after a brief rule the whole thing will come apart. During the reign of Antichrist tensions will mount, and once again the world will explode—with a gigantic world war of overwhelming ferocity involving conflict and massacre on an unparalleled scale. Even the iron grip of the Antichrist will be unable to prevent it. This massive upheaval will be the world's last war—the Battle of Armageddon.

The Battle of Armageddon (and the events leading up to it) will usher in the most intensive suffering known to mankind. In the Bible we read that the earth will be ravaged by political, economic and ecological crises beyond the realm of our imagination. If it were not for the merciful intervention of God, the Bible teaches, the whole world would be destroyed.

Christ—the Victor

In the midst of that whole, terrible, awful carnage described in many parts of the Bible, especially the Book of Revelation, Christ will return as the King of kings and Lord of lords. He Himself will defeat the Antichrist and be the victor of the Battle of Armageddon. At that climactic moment God will set up His Kingdom—a whole new social and political order under His rule.

When Jesus Christ left His followers, he assured His disciples, "I will return!" And He is going to keep that promise. This is our hope.

I remember meeting Sir Winston Churchill during his last year as Prime Minister of Great Britain. It was in London just after one of our Wembley Stadium Crusades. During the course of our conversation Sir Winston had three afternoon newspapers beside him and an unlighted cigar in his mouth. And he said, "Young man, I want to ask you a question. I don't think that the world has very much longer to go. It's in so many troubles." He paused and asked, "Can you give an old man some hope?" I pulled out my New Testament, and I not only gave him the plan of salvation, but I told him all about the return of Christ.

When I was sixteen, I was in revolt against church attendance. I attended because my parents expected me to go, but I could not wait to get away from home and having to go to church and Sunday school each week. An evangelist came to our town. I was not well acquainted with evangelists because our church did not normally cooperate with traveling evangelists. However, there had been a great deal in the press about this particular evangelist, and one night, after he had been there several weeks, I went to hear him at the invitation of a friend. He spoke on the Second Coming of Jesus Christ. This turned out to be one of the major themes of his preaching. It absolutely fascinated me. I had never heard much about it. I never knew there was such a hope and that God had such marvelous things in store for those of the human race who believe.

When is it going to happen? Is the present age drawing to a close? Is the kingdom age soon to be ushered in? I cannot give you any date; Jesus warned us that we were not to try to fix any exact time. History proves how easily we can be mistaken. When Napoleon was sweeping across Europe in the last century many Bible students thought he was the Antichrist. Many people thought Mussolini or Hitler was the Antichrist. They were anti-Christian, but they were not the great Antichrist who is yet to come. The Bible teaches that some day Jesus Christ is coming back to earth. The Scripture holds out both hope and warning.

God is just: He will pay back trouble to those who trouble you and give relief to you who are troubled, and to us as well. This will happen when the Lord Jesus is revealed from heaven in blazing fire with his powerful angels. He will punish those who do not know God and do not obey the gospel of our Lord Jesus. They will be punished with everlasting destruction and shut out from the presence of the Lord and from the majesty of his power on the day he comes to be glorified in his holy people and to be marveled at among all those who have believed (2 Thess. 1:6–10).

The very fact that believers have the hope of the coming of Christ should make us live for Christ every day as though He were coming at any moment. For those who do not know God, the coming of Christ should drive them to Him for forgiveness while there is yet time. This passage also indicates that those who disobey the gospel will get a glimpse of Jesus

Christ in all of His glory, and then be banished from His presence forever. This will be the hell of hell—for a person to carry into eternity the memory of what he missed by deliberately rejecting God's offer of love, mercy and grace in this present life.

After Armageddon

There is a utopia coming. We pray in our churches, "Thy kingdom come. Thy will be done in earth, as *it is* in heaven" (Matt. 6:10, KJV). At the return of Christ, that prayer will be fully realized.

What will happen when the Messiah returns? The Bible teaches us that, in the aftermath of Armageddon, Jesus Christ will establish His reign upon the earth. This will be the greatest spiritual and moral revolution in history as Christ takes control and establishes His reign of righteousness in the world.

This is not a book of prophecy. There are many differing theological viewpoints extant about the future, but this is not the place to debate them. Nevertheless, there are several generalizations we can make about the future state of the world under the reign of Christ.

First, when Christ comes back, Satan is going to be bound. The Bible says, "And I saw an angel coming down out of heaven, having the key to the Abyss and holding in his hand a great chain. He seized the dragon, that ancient serpent, who is the devil, or Satan, . . . He threw him into the Abyss . . . to keep him from deceiving the nations any more" (Rev. 20:1-3). The nations today are being deceived on a grand scale, and the devil is doing it. He is causing them to believe "a lie"—and he is deceiving individuals too. He is telling us that the "broad road" is the right one. But the Bible warns: "There is a way that seems right to a man, but in the end it leads to death" (Prov. 14:12). The devil also is telling people that they have plenty of time to make up their minds about God, eternity and Christ. He is telling them that they don't need God at all—that they can get along without Christ. He is telling us that we can go to heaven without being born again. Jesus said you can't. The devil is saying that there is more pleasure in the world than there is in following Christ. There is not. It will be a glorious day when Satan is bound. No longer will he be able to deceive you and your family and the nations of the world.

Second, during Christ's reign there will be universal justice and peace. There is no such thing as absolute justice in the world today. Economic and social injustices stubbornly resist the best efforts of men and governments to uproot them. The headlines every day tell us there also is no such thing as lasting peace in our world, in spite of countless peace conferences.

But some day justice and peace will be established among all people. The Bible promises, "See, a king will reign in righteousness" (Isa. 32:1). It also tells us, "He will be called . . . Prince of Peace. Of the increase of his government and peace there will be no end" (Isa. 9:6,7).

One day, shortly after the United Nations building had been erected on the banks of the East River in New York City, I was taken on a tour of the building by an ambassador friend from another country. He showed me an empty room. He said, "This is the prayer room." It was absolutely empty: there was no symbol, nothing to indicate that there was any God at all. When the United Nations was founded it was agreed the word *God* should be left out of its charter. The world has left God out of its planning.

But all that is going to be changed. When Jesus comes back He is coming not as the lowly Nazarene carpenter riding on a donkey. He is coming in divine majesty and power and glory. He is coming as a Prince, as a King, with thousands of His angel-warriors with Him. The mightiest army the universe has ever known will be arrayed. And though the Antichrist will declare war on Him, the victory will be His. Emerging triumphant from the smoke of that last terrible, awful war will be the Messiah, the Lord Jesus Christ, the Prince of Peace.

When Jesus comes back we will know safety and security. Do you know what George Washington's favorite verse of Scripture was? It was Micah 4:4; he quoted it constantly. "Every man will sit under his own vine and under his own fig tree, and no one will make them afraid, for the Lord Almighty has spoken."

During Christ's reign, political confusion will be turned to order and harmony, social injustices will be abolished, and moral corruption will be replaced by integrity. For the first time in history the whole world will know what it is like to live in a society governed by God's principles. And Satan's influence will not be present to hinder world progress toward peace, unity, equality, and justice. Man's dream for global harmony will be realized!

Finally, the Bible teaches us that when Christ comes again every person who has ever lived will stand before God's judgment.

When those who have repented of their sin in rebellion against God and accepted Jesus as their Savior and the Lord of their lives appear before God, He will usher them into their new home—heaven and all its glories. This will be the Garden of Eden restored. Men will see God face to face and live with Him in an environment free of fears, failures, and fatigue.

But those who chose to reject God during their lifetime on earth will be separated from Him for eternity. This is not God's desire, but man's own choice. God holds every man accountable for his rejection of Christ.

God does not want men to separate themselves from Him eternally. At the same time, God will not force a man to live in heaven against his will. In 2 Peter 3:9 the apostle says that God is "patient . . . not wanting anyone to perish, but everyone to come to repentance." John 3:16 says, "God so loved the world that he gave his *one and only* Son, that whoever believes in him shall not perish but have eternal life" (italics mine). At great cost to Himself, God has made it possible for each of us to live with Him eternally. Those who reject God's offer of a heavenly home will be assigned to hell.

When we are called before God and His throne of judgment, it will be too late to reverse our decision. It is during our lifetime here on earth that we decide our eternal destiny.

Till Armageddon

We have had a glimpse of the future—both its horror and its hope. But what about the present? How do we prepare for the suffering we may possibly have to face as our world moves relentlessly toward a period of intense tribulation—to be climaxed at Armageddon? And how do we prepare for the daily armageddons we each face, the problems and suffering that are part of every human life? Whether or not Christians will actually have to face the period of tribulation around Armageddon is a matter of debate among equally sincere Bible scholars. But there can be no doubt that suffering in one form or another comes to us all. And we can be certain that God will give us the strength and resources we need to live through any situation in life that He ordains. The will of God will never take us where the grace of God cannot sustain us. As we shall see in the pages that follow, God is also able to take every situation in life—no matter how difficult—and use it to draw us closer to Himself.

Because suffering is a natural part of human existence, we must learn to cope with it. And for the Christian, in particular, there seems to be a unique set of sufferings. God wants us to learn how to deal with our trials and temptations in dependence on His power. The Bible and the history of the church both demonstrate that God's way for the suffering of His people has not always been the way of escape, but the way of endurance.

But how can we endure the crises of death, persecution, or physical illness? How do we cope with the heartaches of family strife, divorce, financial burdens? How do we live through the tensions of a world crowded with national disasters and social injustices?

That is what this book is about. It is a book about suffering, and how to deal with it. When Christ returns as the victor at Armageddon, suffering will be abolished. *Till Armageddon* we must learn to live triumphantly amid the traumas and pressures we face daily. We must prepare for our own personal armageddons.

*The Lord gets his best soldiers out
of the highlands of affliction.*
CHARLES HADDON SPURGEON

2/

Personal Armageddons

Suffering Is Universal

We don't deliberately look for trouble in life. It comes. Suffering is a universal fact; no one can escape its claws. The rain falls upon the just and the unjust. We all face personal armageddons.

Some people have the mistaken idea that becoming a Christian will be a shelter from the personal storms of life. The story of many of our hymns will swiftly dispel this myth. A large number of our favorite hymns and spiritual songs were composed in the crucible of life.

Many illustrations could be given. Charlotte Elliott wrote "Just As I Am" when she was a helpless invalid. Frances Ridley Havergal, author of "Take My Life" and many other hymns, suffered much ill health. Fanny Crosby was blind, yet out of her suffering came such lovely songs as "Safe in the Arms of Jesus." The hymn "God Moves in a Mysterious Way" was composed by the poet William Cowper in an hour of great mental distress.

One of the most frequently read portions of the Bible is the Book of Psalms. We turn to them so often because of the wide range of moods and experiences they represent. We can relate to them and find comfort in them because they reflect real life, with its joys and sorrows. Many of the Psalms were produced during periods of national and personal crises.

Psalm 137 expresses the heartache and agony of a people banished from their native land:

> By the rivers of Babylon we sat and
> wept
> when we remembered Zion.
> There on the poplars
> we hung our harps.
> (Ps. 137:1,2)

After ravaging the land of Israel, the Babylonian army had forced its captives to march toward a land of exile and a terrifying future. Depressed and forlorn, the Hebrews discarded their musical instruments. There was no song left in their hearts. This Psalm keenly captures the feelings of a refugee people.

Many of the Psalms reflect the personal crises faced by David, Israel's greatest king. We regard him as a man of unbelievable successes—his youthful triumph over the Philistine giant Goliath, his remarkable rise from shepherd boy to monarch, his notable victories over Israel's foes. But David was also a man of unbearable sorrow. Unjustly accused of treason, he was forced to live for years as a fugitive. One of his sons died in infancy, some were morally corrupt, others were ruthlessly murdered. At one point in his kingship, his own nation turned against him as another son attempted a coup.

God called David "a man after [my] own heart" (1 Sam. 13:14). Although God obviously loved David, He did not exempt him from suffering.

No one is exempt from the touch of tragedy: neither the Christian nor the non-Christian; neither the rich nor the poor; neither the leader nor the commoner. Crossing all racial, social, political, and economic barriers, suffering reaches out to unite mankind.

The Reality of Suffering

Suffering is difficult to talk or write about, for it is not something that can adequately be examined outside the realm of experience. It is not abstract, nor is it philosophical. It is real and concrete. It leaves its scars. When the winds of adversity have passed, we are seldom unchanged.

It is only when one has passed through a crisis event that one can truly comprehend what it means to suffer. And often it is only in retrospect that we realize the purpose and value of our suffering.

Have you ever noticed that those who make the greatest impact upon society are often those who have suffered most?

Suffering in life can uncover untold depths of character and unknown strength for service. People who go through life unscathed by sorrow and untouched by pain tend to be shallow in their perspective on life. Suffering, on the other hand, tends to plow up the surface of our lives to uncover the depths that provide greater strength of purpose and accomplishment. Only deeply plowed earth can yield bountiful harvests.

Pain has many faces. One can suffer physically, mentally, emotionally, psychologically, and spiritually. Our difficulties are rarely confined to only one of these areas; they tend to overlap in human experiences. Some of the most intensive suffering can be psychologically induced and frequently lead to complications in the physical realm.

There are as many invisible hurts as there are visible hurts, and there can be difficulty in diagnosing them. We know that the unseen part of man is often the victim of the most debilitating of pains. In certain circumstances, a man can endure excruciating physical pain; and yet he can be felled by one unkind word. When we hear the story of the torture inflicted upon a P.O.W., we are astounded by his personal fortitude and the resiliency of the human body. But that same man's life can be devastated by a single viciously perpetrated act or word.

Scripture has much to say about the power of the tongue to inflict cruelty. The psalmist says that bitter words are like deadly arrows. James wrote: "The tongue is a small part of the body, but it makes great boasts. Consider what a great forest is set on fire by a small spark. The tongue also is a fire, a world of evil among the parts of the body" (James 3:5,6).

Man is capable of great victories and susceptible to great defeats. Man is both strong and sensitive. As the psalmist exclaimed, "I praise you because I am fearfully and wonderfully made" (Ps. 139:14).

In earnest we must endeavor to apply this sensitivity when dealing with the matter of suffering, especially as we consider the sufferings of others. We cannot feel someone else's pain. We can see the anguish in his face and try to empathize. But we do not have his nerve endings. We cannot fully know the magnitude of his anguish. We must never minimize the suffering of another. Scripture's mandate to us is, "Weep with them that weep" (Rom. 12:15, kjv).

Our physical sufferings express a great truth. As C. S. Lewis cogently penned, "Pain . . . plants the flag of truth within the fortress of a rebel soul."[1] The truth is this—man's body is mortal, temporal. Man must look beyond himself to find immortality.

Suffering is one of God's ways of speaking to us, of awakening us to our need of Him, and calling us to Himself. To quote C. S. Lewis again: "God whispers to us in our pleasures, speaks in our conscience, but shouts in our pains: it is His megaphone to rouse a deaf world."[2] If our suffering leads us to God, it has become a blessed and precious friend.

We are indebted to modern medical science for the tremendous strides made in finding cures for so many diseases and harnessing others. Through dedicated efforts, progress is being made daily in the discovery of new ways of relieving the physical sufferings of mankind. Many lives have been saved and are now being sustained as a result of such scientific advances.

And yet pain is still with us. Many of you know the reality of cancer, strokes, heart attacks, birth defects, auto injuries. Many of you have been bedridden and racked with pain for years. Some of you are shocked by the discovery of a friend's or relative's terminal illness. Maybe you yourself are facing the prospect of death. Let me assure you that you do not need to face your situation alone. God wants to comfort and help you.

Some suffering comes as a natural result of the deterioration

---

1. C. S. Lewis, *The Problem of Pain* (New York: The Macmillan Co., 1955), p. 83.
2. Ibid., p. 81.

of the body. Some forms of physical suffering are inflicted upon us by others.

Throughout the history of Christianity, followers of Christ have suffered persecution. In an African country a young Christian school principal was dragged from his office into the street where he was about to be shot. The curious townspeople crowded one side of the street and the school children the other. The young principal asked his captors if he could have just a few minutes, and when they granted his request he sang out: "Out of my bondage, sorrow and night, Jesus, I come; Jesus, I come," after which he was shot. The blood of the martyrs is the seed of the church. While Christians in America have worshiped without the fear or threat of physical abuse for their beliefs, thousands of their brothers in Christ throughout the world have been tortured and martyred for confessing the name of Christ.

There may come a day when we Americans will undergo intense persecution for our faith. Are you prepared to face martyrdom? Jesus gave His life for you. You may be called to give your life for Him. God has many precious promises for those who suffer for Christ. We will be looking at these later in this book.

Mental Suffering

E. Stanley Jones tells the story of a minister who was preparing a series of ten sermons on the topic, "How to Avoid Having a Nervous Breakdown." Before his work was completed, he himself had a breakdown. The pressure of trying to meet the deadline was too great for him.

All of us experience some form of mental anxiety during our lifetimes. The spectrum of mental suffering is wide, ranging from the worry experienced by a young person anticipating a blind date to the nervous breakdown of a corporation executive.

We are all susceptible to depression—and Christians are no exception.

Elijah, that dynamic and dedicated prophet of God, valiantly and effectively defended the cause of God in terrifying confrontations with paganism. Elijah rose to great heights of faith as he withstood the continued threats of vile King Ahab and his vicious wife, Jezebel (1 Kings 19). But there came a point in his life when he wanted to give up entirely. Even the simple demands in life became *too great to bear.* "It is enough;" he said, "now, O Lord, take away my life" (v.4, KJV). He was overwhelmed by a combination of exhaustion and depression.

God did not grant his request, nor did He remonstrate with him. God knew that Elijah was suffering from exhaustion and depression and gave him what he needed: sleep and food, and the reassurance that he was not alone. God saw the root of Elijah's problem: he had expended his physical and mental resources. He had gone beyond his breaking point. Someone has said, "How many problems are solved by a good night's sleep." But the ones that are still with us when we wake up need the special touch of God.

Another important figure in the history of Christianity suffered in a similar fashion. Toward the end of a popular and flourishing ministry, John the Baptist was imprisoned by Herod Antipas, the governor of Galilee. John, the man of the desert with its wide open spaces and unending stretch of sky, lay in a dark, dank dungeon.

During his imprisonment John's faith was shaken to its very roots. This was the same John who had said, "Behold, the Lamb of God, which taketh away the sin of the world" (John 1:29, KJV).

What had caused him to question?

He had understood when some of his disciples had left him to follow Jesus. Then he had denounced Herod for living with his brother's wife, and was thrown in prison. Matthew tells us, "Now when John had heard in the prison the works of Christ, he sent two of his disciples, And said unto him, Art thou he that should come, or do we look for another?" (Matt. 11:2,3, KJV).

What had John heard? What works of Jesus? Had he heard that He had eaten with publicans and sinners? That He had been compassionate toward a woman taken in adultery—the very sin, the denouncing of which had landed John in prison? Or had he heard of His miracles?

Jesus could have rescued John, and he hadn't; no word had

been raised in protest over Herod's action; the unopened prison—unexplained. Perhaps it was everything combined that caused John's faith to waver.

Our Lord's reply to the distressed prophet is most notable. After reassuring John regarding His identity, He praised both John and his ministry (Matt. 11:1–11). Vance Havner has made this instructive observation regarding the episode: "When John said his worst about Jesus, Jesus said His best about John."

Depressed people need reassurance and encouragement. Jesus knew this and practiced it. We can learn much from the way God dealt with Elijah and from Jesus' dealings with John. They can serve as our models for ministering to those burdened by mental anxieties. People in distress need a gentle, helping hand and words of encouragement.

Christians are particularly susceptible to exhaustion that leads to depression. With a sense of dedication to God that inspires them to work diligently for His kingdom, they often assume overwhelming tasks and ignore warning signs. With no one else to assist, and seeing a job to be done, they overwork themselves and fall prey to depression.

Those in roles of Christian leadership need to be alert to such cases.

Each of us has his own unique, God-given set of abilities and talents—his own personal potential for accomplishment. Not all of us work at the same speed or reach the same heights. God does not want us to compete against each other. He wants us to compete against ourselves—to learn to work within our own individual capacities.

Jesus told a parable in which He taught that one day every Christian's accomplishments would be evaluated by Him personally. Jesus explained that He would judge a man, not by what he does in comparison with others, but by what he does with the capabilities God has given him.

God has given each of us special abilities and potentials *and certain limitations*. Let us develop our abilities and strive to work toward our potentials. But let us learn where our breaking points lie. Sometimes it is simply a matter of moving forward, stopping for a rest, and then continuing.

A well-tuned machine gives the best performance. A well-tuned, balanced Christian life will be the most productive for the kingdom of God.

Emotional and Psychological Suffering

All of us suffer disappointments in life. Sometimes the effect upon us can be minor. At other times our lives can be devastated.

Loneliness, for instance, may be so intense that proper functioning as a man or woman is almost impossible. Shortly after her beloved consort Prince Albert died, Queen Victoria is reported to have confided in her trusted friend, Dean Stanley, that she was "always wishing to consult one who is not here, groping by myself, with a constant sense of desolation."

Many of you are suffering from *rejection,* a hurt which causes great damage, for it affects us deep within. Possibly a girl friend or boy friend has dropped you for someone else. Or your marriage is breaking up over a third party. Possibly you have been interviewed for an important job and been turned down.

We see so many emotional and psychological sufferings among our young people today. The chief cause of death among college students is *suicide.* The current generation may face greater pressures than any other generation in modern times. Academically, students compete at the undergraduate level for elite positions in graduate school. One of our leading medical schools, to which only the most highly qualified apply, has only one position available for every 400 applicants. One has to be incredibly strong to withstand this type of competition.

Many students find themselves in the midst of preparing for a future in a particular career only to face a declining job market.

The cost of education is increasing, forcing many students to bear the responsibility of working while they are at school.

By and large, in recent decades our society has discouraged our youth from looking to God for help. Without God as a source of guidance and strength, youth have turned to escapism through drugs, which has created new and deep-seated problems.

Insecurities can be crippling. We have fears that plague us and keep us from stepping out on new adventures and striving after new accomplishments. Often we hesitate to be aggressive in situations because we fear failure. There may be a job to do, but we do not feel adequate or qualified. Or we feel that we cannot do as good a job as our predecessor.

How would you feel stepping into the shoes of Moses, that man of miracles whom God chose to lead the Hebrew people out of Egyptian bondage? Apparently Joshua, Moses' well-trained apprentice who was to lead the Israelites into the Promised Land, experienced a great sense of insecurity. During one particular "pep talk" with the new leader, God had to tell him three times not to be afraid. And the third time, God explained why Joshua could begin his new respon-sibilities with confidence:

> Have I not commanded you? Be strong and courageous. Do not be terrified; do not be discouraged, *for the Lord your God will be with you wherever you go* (Josh. 1:9, italics mine).

God promised His presence. And where God is, there also we find His peace and His power—a power which enables us to rise above discouragement and which leads us through the defeats in life. As we shall see, God can even use our disappointments to bring good into our lives. God does not call us to be successful, but to be obedient.

We must remember that we *are* weak vessels, through whom God can channel His power to accomplish *His* purposes. As one conference speaker is often heard saying, "God, I can't; but you can, so let's go!"

Emotional and psychological problems can result from things that come into our lives. But we can also be crippled by those things which do not come into our lives.

Some people are emotionally disabled because of an ab-sence of love in their lives—particularly in their childhood. Those who have not received love in their early life find it difficult to give love later on. Nevertheless, regardless of how twisted and disordered our lives may be, God is able to bring us peace and He can put the pattern back into our lives.

Spiritual Sufferings

Not all pain is destructive. There is a sense in which pain acts as a warning system, alerting us that medical assistance is needed. This can also be true spiritually.

These are times when we agonize over unconfessed sin in our lives. Our guilt erupts in tense relationships, nervous habits, sleepless nights. Our consciences are heavily burdened until we come to the Great Physician for healing. "If we confess our sins, he is faithful and just and will forgive us our sins and purify us from all unrighteousness" (1 John 1:9).

The struggle against sin can produce a form of suffering. The Bible speaks of this as a battle. But we do not go into the battle defenseless. God equips us with His "full armor" (Eph. 6:13). Jesus can release us from the power of Satan and sin. We are not compelled to go the way of our temptations. But God expects us to fight. God does not promise to take the battle from us, but to take us through the battle.

When we become Christians we gain a Friend, the Lord Jesus Christ. But we also gain an enemy—Satan. Satan attempts to lure us from the path of spiritual progress. And he seeks to destroy our ministries.

But we must remember this. First, Satan is *not* omnipotent. He is not God's equal. He is a fallen angel, not a fallen god. Second, nothing can come into our lives without God's knowledge and permission. Satan is actually under God's authority. He had to receive God's permission to test Job. Third, God can produce good out of the trials and afflictions that Satan tries to put in the Christian's path.

The Gospels record an episode in Jesus' life in which He was in the midst of a teaching session in a synagogue. Unexpectedly, a demon-possessed man jumped to his feet and began yelling. You see, Satan was trying to disrupt the session, for he did not want Jesus' audience to learn about the kingdom of God and the truths of eternal life. Immediately Jesus cast out the demon, thus demonstrating His complete authority over the spiritual world. His audience, already impressed by His teaching, was now doubly impressed by His power (Mark 1:21–27). What Satan tried to do to hinder Jesus, actually helped Him.

Satan must be the most frustrated personality in the universe! His army of demons is compelled to obey Jesus, and whatever the devil does to discourage a Christian, God can use for the Christian's benefit. Sometimes He allows us to suffer so that we may grow spiritually.

Most often suffering cannot be accurately or fully understood except in retrospect. Not until time has ceased and eternity begun will Job understand why God allowed him to be tested as he was. Not until then will the challenging and comforting role that he has played through the centuries in countless thousands of lives be fully known.

God Wants to Help You

Recently, science has devised a remarkable machine, the body scanner, which can detect disorders in the body which evade even the X-ray. Sometimes we have hurts that are too deep and sensitive for others to see or help.

But who except God Himself can scan the invisible me—my heart, my soul, my spirit? There are hurts in our personalities too deep and too complicated for even the most sophisticated modern techniques to diagnose or to solve.

Only God Himself who made us understands us fully. As the psalmist said, "O Lord, you have searched me and you know me. You know when I sit and when I rise; you perceive my thoughts from afar" (Ps. 139:1,2). Only God can diagnose our problem accurately and will show us how to solve it; and when there is no solution, He will give us the grace to live with it. Only God can answer our question, "Why?" and when there is no answer, give us His peace and grace to live with "the unanswered."

God wants to help us when we suffer. He can give His *presence* for comfort, His *power* for endurance, His *purpose* so that we might gain insight into our situation. And He can produce within us valuable qualities that will strengthen and mold our lives.

God can help us because He alone knows *why* we are suffering and *where* the suffering can take us.

He can also help us because *He* knows *what* it means to suffer. When we go through difficult times and turn to someone for counsel and comfort, we seek someone who can understand—someone who has experienced a similar situation and can relate to our feelings.

God can relate to us because He has suffered in the person of His Son.

The Son of God left the realms of heaven, became a man, and lived for thirty-three years in a suffering world. He ministered to suffering people. He encountered all types of physical, mental, emotional, psychological, and spiritual problems—and He demonstrated His ability to deal with each one. Your problem is not new to the Lord Jesus Christ. He is neither surprised nor baffled by it.

Jesus not only saw the sufferings of others—He Himself suffered. He experienced the same trials and temptations as you face.

He knew *physical* suffering. At times, He found His ministry physically exhausting and needed to seek refreshment. As far as experiencing intense physical pain, He endured a cruel torture and painful death: flogging and crucifixion. He knew *mental, emotional,* and *psychological* suffering. So often He experienced personal *rejection.* His brothers mocked Him and His ministry. When He preached in His hometown, the crowd ran Him out of the village and even tried to kill Him. Eventually the religious leaders of His own nation plotted His death.

And Jesus experienced *loneliness.* At times even His own chosen apostles completely misunderstood Him. Who could fully relate in a friendship to someone who was both God and man? After a long day of demanding work, Jesus had no wife and family to whom He could return and find comfort and encouragement.

And imagine the trauma of leaving the environment of heaven, where He was recognized and revered as the Son of God by thousands of angels—and coming to a sin-marred earth where He was met with scorn and contempt.

Jesus knew *spiritual* suffering. At the beginning of His

public ministry Satan tempted Him unmercifully for forty days. And Satan returned throughout Jesus' ministry to try to defeat the Son of God and deflect Him from His mission. Jesus withstood him and won the battle.

And Jesus experienced a spiritual suffering more intense than you and I will ever know. For a period of time while He was on the cross, He experienced the horror of separation from God and cried, "My God, my God, why have you forsaken me?" For Jesus, this was the greatest agony of all. To be forsaken by the Father who loved Him—to have the Father turn His back on the Son—this was the supreme suffering, the ultimate penalty for sin. You and I, if we have received Christ as Savior, will never have to be separated from God, because Jesus paid that penalty for sin. This is why Paul could so confidently claim:

> For I am convinced that neither death nor life, neither angels nor demons, neither the present nor the future, nor any powers, neither height nor depth, nor anything else in all creation, will be able to separate us from the love of God that is in Christ Jesus our Lord (Rom. 8:38,39).

Nothing will ever separate us from God! Because Jesus, in His suffering, was separated from God on our behalf, we now have *eternal life* through trusting in Him as Savior.

So the Son of God can relate to us in our hour of need. He can relate to our suffering—He can do something for us. As Thomas Moore's hymn so beautifully expresses:

> Come, ye disconsolate, where'er ye languish;
> Come to the mercy seat, fervently kneel;
> Here bring your wounded hearts, here tell your anguish;
> *Earth has no sorrow that heaven cannot heal.*[3]

God wants to help us. You may be going through difficulties right now. Or possibly your life is currently free from tragedy. Regardless of your particular circumstances, it is important to

---

3. Italics mine.

prepare for suffering. Suffering rarely makes a reservation ahead of time.

This book will explore ways in which you can prepare for your personal armageddons by understanding biblical teachings on suffering.

Now, if you are someone for whom a personal relationship with God is a new concept, if you do not know the reality of the living God taking up residence within your life, if you have never confessed your sins and received Jesus Christ as your Lord and Savior, I want to personally invite you to do this now.

This is the first step in getting God's help. He wants to heal you on the inside. He wants to cure your deepest problem first—the problem of personal sin.

Confess your sin, receive Jesus as your Savior—and then begin a new life with Him. You will find God's peace in your heart, His guidance in your life, and the comfort of His presence through your suffering—through your personal armageddon, whatever form it may take.

God measures out affliction to our need.

ST. JOHN CHRYSOSTOM

3/

Who's in Charge of a World That Suffers?

WE HAVE REACHED a dilemma. The world seems to be careening toward destruction. We see the innocent suffer and the good person experience pain and anguish. The voices of the doubters and skeptics are heard asking, "What kind of a God allows these things to happen?"

Are we helplessly propelled by fate toward our destiny, or is there a Supreme Being in control?

We were recently viewing some photographs which our son brought back with him from Cambodia. One looked like a circular flower bed, with a two-foot-high brick border surrounding it. Poles held up a thatched roof, very much like an old-fashioned summer pavilion. This giant container held nothing but human skulls—victims of some of the most mindless brutality the world has ever known.

He had another picture of a lovely young girl, but where her eyes should have been there were only holes. They had been gouged out by the enemy.

Who's in charge?

We have just read a little book by Laurel Lee, the author of *Walking Through the Fire*. This lovely young girl discovered during her third month of pregnancy that she had Hodgkin's disease. The doctors wanted to perform an abortion, since she would be required to take cobalt treatments. She refused to have an abortion, but went through with the treatments. Her husband, unable to face the prospect of raising three children without a wife, left her, divorced her and married someone else.

With her childlike faith in God, her brilliant mind, and delightful sense of humor, she proceeded to write a diary of her experiences, illustrating them as she went along. One of the doctors came across it and sent it to a publisher in New York. This led to a new phase of her life, a public ministry with speaking engagements. Soon she and her children had a little home of their own. The disease seemed to have gone into remission. Some time passed, and the disease cropped up again. Facing death, Laurel Lee has come out with a new book, *Signs of Spring*. At times she must have wondered if God was in control.

There are millions of people throughout the world who are suffering from injustice, political oppression, or persecution who must ask, "Why is this happening? Who's in control?" There are thousands of homes with broken and shattered lives. The entire world seems to be a hospital, a mortuary, or a graveyard, with people asking the same question, "Who is in control?"

Scientists and philosophers throughout the ages have debated the existence or nonexistence of God. Today, however, the evidence is so overwhelming that even the intellectual doubters are beginning to reason that there is a Supreme Being.

Time magazine had an article called "Modernizing the Case for God" (April 7, 1980, p. 65). It said, "In a quiet revolution in thought and argument that hardly anyone could have foreseen only two decades ago, God is making a comeback. Most intriguingly, this is happening not among theologians or ordinary believers—most of whom never accepted for a moment that he was in any serious trouble—but in the crisp, intellectual circles of academic philosophers."

We have come full circle from Romans 1 back to Romans 1. The Bible says, "Since the creation of the world God's invisible qualities—his eternal power and divine nature—have been clearly seen, being understood from what has been made, so that men are without excuse" (Rom. 1:20).

What Is God Like?

A simple, straightforward answer to this very basic question is hard to find—unless we simply remind ourselves that God is just like Jesus Christ! All the attributes of God are seen in Jesus Christ: His love, mercy, compassion, purity, sovereignty, and might. This is why our faith in God must always be Christ-centered. As Dr. Michael Ramsey, the former Archbishop of Canterbury, wrote: "The heart of Christian doctrine is not only that Jesus is divine, but that God is Christlike and in him is no un-Christlikeness at all."[1]

The greatness of God defies the limitations of language.

As I read the Bible, I seem to find *holiness* to be His supreme attribute. However, *love* is also a prime quality. The promises of God's love and forgiveness are as real, as sure, as positive, as human words can describe. God is holy love.

Behind the love of God lies His omniscience—His ability to "know and understand all." Omniscience is that quality of God which is His alone. God possesses infinite knowledge and an awareness which is uniquely His. At all times, even in the midst of any type of suffering, I can realize that He knows, loves, watches, understands, and, more than that, He has a purpose.

As a boy I grew up in the South. My idea of the ocean was so small that the first time I saw the Atlantic I couldn't comprehend that any little lake could be so big! The vastness of the ocean cannot be understood until it is seen. This is the same with God's love. It passes knowledge. Until you actually experience it, no one can describe its wonders to you.

A good illustration of this is a story my wife told me about a man in China who was selling cherries. Along came a little boy who loved cherries; and when he saw the fruit, his eyes filled with longing. But he had no money with which to buy cherries.

---

1. *God, Christ and the World* (London: SCM Press, 1969), p. 37.

The kindly seller asked the boy, "Do you want some cherries?" And the little boy said that he did.

The seller said, "Hold out your hands." But the little boy didn't hold out his hands. The seller said again, "Hold out your hands," but again the little boy would not. The kind seller reached down, took the child's hands, filled them with two handfuls of cherries.

Later, the boy's grandmother heard of the incident and asked, "Why didn't you hold out your hands when he asked you to?" And the little boy answered, "His hands are bigger than mine!"

God's hands, also, are bigger than ours!

Some of our modern experts in theology have made attempts to rob God of His warmth, His deep love for mankind, and His sympathy for His creatures. But God's love is unchangeable. He loves us in spite of knowing us as we really are. In fact, He created us because He wanted other creatures in His image in the universe upon whom He could pour out His love, and who, in turn, would voluntarily love Him. He wanted people with the ability to say "yes" or "no" in their relationship to Him. Love is not satisfied with an automaton—one who has no choice but to love and obey. Not mechanized love, but voluntary love satisfies the heart of God.

Were it not for the love of God, none of us would ever have a chance in the future life!

Some years ago a friend of mine was standing on top of a mountain in North Carolina. The roads in those days were filled with curves, and it was difficult to see very far ahead. This man saw two cars heading toward each other. He realized that they couldn't see each other. A third car pulled up and began to pass one of the cars, although there wasn't enough space to see the other car approaching around the bend. My friend shouted a warning, but the drivers couldn't hear, and there was a fatal crash. The man on the mountain saw it all.

This is how God looks upon us in His omniscience. He sees what has happened, what is happening, and what will happen. In the Scriptures He warns us time after time about troubles, problems, sufferings, and judgment that lie ahead. Many times we ignore His warnings.

God sees all and knows all. But we are too limited by the

finiteness of our minds and the short time we have on earth even to begin to understand the mighty God and the universe He has created.

He Is a God of Love

God is not blind to man's plight. He does not stand on a mountaintop, helplessly viewing the crash of mankind. Since man caused his own crash by his rebellion against the Creator, God could have allowed him to plunge on in darkness and destruction. This would have been in keeping with God's holiness and righteousness. However, this other great attribute of God, His love, would not allow Him to do it. From the very beginning of that crash, God had a plan for man's deliverance, redemption and reconciliation. In fact the plan is so fantastic that it ultimately lifts man far beyond and above even the angels. God's all-consuming love for mankind was decisively demonstrated at the cross, where His compassion was embodied in His Son Jesus Christ. The word *compassion* comes from two Latin words meaning "to suffer with." God was willing to suffer with man.

In the thirty-three years preceding His death, Jesus suffered *with* man; on the cross He suffered *for* man. "God was reconciling the world to himself in Christ" (2 Cor. 5:19). Again, "God demonstrates his own love for us in this: While we were still sinners, Christ died for us" (Rom. 5:8).

It was the love of God that sent Jesus Christ to the cross. It was because He was in control and controlled by *love* that He provided that divine substitute for our sin.

God's love did not begin at the cross. It began before the world was established, before the time clock of civilization began to move. The concept stretches our understanding to the utmost limits of our minds.

Turn back in your imaginations to the countless eons before God created this present earth, when it was "without form and void" and the deep, silent darkness of outer space formed a vast gulf between the brilliance of God's throne and the dark vacuum where our present solar system now exists. Imagine the brilliance of God's glory as the cherubim and seraphim, the very angels themselves, cover their faces with their wings in awe and reverence toward Him who is the high and holy One who inhabits eternity!

Even at this time He foreknew all that would happen, and yet, in His mysterious love He allowed it. The Bible tells us about the "Lamb that was slain from the creation of the world" (Rev. 13:8). God foresaw what His Son was to suffer. As it has been said, there was a cross in the heart of God long before the cross was erected at Calvary. Only as we think in these terms will we begin to grasp the wonder and greatness of His love for us.

His Love, As Time Begins

It was love that prompted God to fashion a creature in His own image, and to place him in a paradise of unsurpassed beauty. It was His love that provided the plan of salvation, for He knew in advance how man would deviate from the original divine program.

It was the love of God which granted to man freedom of will and the privilege of choice when He said: "You are free to eat from any tree in the garden; but you must not eat from the tree of the knowledge of good and evil, for when you eat of it you will surely die" (Gen. 2:16,17). Only God gives His children freedom of choice. Man was liberated from the beginning of time to do his own thing, but whatever his choice, there were to be consequences. If he chose rebellion, there would be terrible suffering, death, and eternal separation from God. If he chose obedience to God's plan of salvation, there would be abundant joy, eternal life, and the eventual building of a paradise on this planet.

God was so concerned for man's welfare that He carefully marked the danger spot in this perfect environment. "Eat of every other tree," said God, "but not of this one. There is death in this one."

But man made a fatal blunder that would affect every generation that would ever be born. In spite of God's warning Adam and Eve ate the fruit of that tree. However, it was the same love which made God call out to Adam, "Where are you?" (Gen. 3:9). God knew where Adam was—but *He wanted Adam to know.* He prepared the way for Adam and Eve to return to Him in fellowship.

It was the love of God which put the Ten Commandments in the hands of His servant, Moses. It was His love which engraved these statutes not only in stone but upon the hearts of all people (upon their consciences) and made them the basis of all civil, statutory, and moral law, no matter how perverted human justice may have become.

It was God's love which knew that men were incapable of obeying His law, and it was His love which promised a Redeemer, a Savior, who would save His people from their sins.

It was the love of God which put words of promise into the mouths and hearts of His prophets centuries before Christ came.

His Love, As Prophecy Is Fulfilled

Just as the ancient prophets foretold, at a certain time in the history of mankind, at a specific place in the Middle East, the Son of God came to this planet.

It was God's love that prepared the political conditions for the coming of Jesus Christ. Greece, as the great power during the four-hundred-year period before the birth of Christ, prepared the way for His message by spreading a common language (Greek) throughout the world. Then the great Roman Empire came into power and built a network of roads and developed a system of law and order. So, by using the common language, plus the Roman roads and legal system, God, through the early Christians, spread His Word. Thus the Scripture says that Jesus was born in "the fulness of the time" (Gal. 4:4, KJV).

One Life, One Love, One God

The Son of God reflects the same selfless compassion for the sick, the distressed, and the sin-burdened, as does God the Father.

It was God's love which enabled Jesus Christ to become

poor, that we might be made rich. It was divine love that enabled Him to endure the Cross. It was this same love which restrained Him when He was falsely accused of blasphemy and was led to Golgotha to die with common thieves, never raising a hand against His enemies.

It was love that kept Him from calling 12,000 angels who had already drawn their swords to come to His rescue. It was that same love which made Him, in a moment of agonizing pain, pause and give life and hope to a repentant sinner dying beside Him who cried, "Jesus, remember me when you come into your kingdom" (Luke 23:42).

After terrible torture had been inflicted upon Him by degenerate man, it was love that caused Him to lift His voice and pray, "Father, forgive them, for they do not know what they are doing" (Luke 23:34).

From Genesis to Revelation, from earth's greatest tragedy to earth's greatest triumph, the dramatic story of man's lowest depths and God's most sublime heights can be expressed in twenty-five tremendous words: "For God so loved the world, that he gave his only begotten Son, that whosoever believeth in him should not perish, but have everlasting life" (John 3:16, KJV).

How Can We Reject So Great a Love?

On the human plane, we frequently love the one who loves us. In the spiritual realm, people do not comprehend the overwhelming love of a holy God. We try to be "good enough for God."

The prophet Isaiah expressed man's true condition in the words, "We all, like sheep, have gone astray, each of us has turned to his own way" (Isa. 53:6).

No matter what sin we have committed, or how heinous, shameful, or terrible it may be, *God loves us.* If we have tried to "live a good life," by our own standards—it is unacceptable to God for salvation. Yet, God loves those, too, whether they are trying to be good or trying to be bad. God's love is all-encompassing.

However, there is one thing God's love cannot do. It cannot forgive the unrepentant sinner. The human race is called on throughout the Bible to repent of sin and rebellion and return to God.

Thus, because of His love there is a way of salvation, a way back to God through Jesus Christ, His Son.

This love of God that reaches to wherever a man is can be entirely rejected. God will not force Himself upon any man against his will. A person can hear a message about the love of God and say, "No, I won't have it," and God will let him go on in his sin to slavery and judgment.

However, if we really want to receive the love of God, *we must accept it for ourselves.* That's the way He planned it from the beginning! It's always been man's choice. The destiny of your own soul is in your own hands by the choice you make.

Have you committed your life to Jesus Christ? Do you know Him as your personal Savior and Lord?

God Is . . . Every Place

I remember reading a booklet with the title, *No Place to Hide.* How well that describes the omnipotence and omniscience of God. "'Can anyone hide in secret places so that I cannot see him?' declares the Lord. 'Do not I fill heaven and earth?' declares the Lord" (Jer. 23:24).

In Psalm 139:1–5, David said, "O Lord, you have searched me and you know me. You know when I sit and when I rise; you perceive my thoughts from afar. You discern my going out and my lying down; you are familiar with all my ways. Before a word is on my tongue you know it completely, O Lord. You hem me in, behind and before; you have laid your hand upon me."

While David could not explain the *manner* of God's omniscient (all-knowing) love, he could tell *how* it affected him: "Such knowledge is too wonderful for me, too lofty for me to attain" (v.6).

The psalmist then goes on to acknowledge that God is, indeed, in every place. "Where can I go from your Spirit? Where can I flee from your presence? If I go up to the heavens, you are there; if I make my bed in the depths, you are there" (vv.7,8).

If one could climb to the highest heights or descend to the

lowest depths, one could not escape the presence of almighty God. This is what the omniscience (all-knowing) and omnipresence (everywhere at once) of God means to us in practical terms. "If I rise on the wings of the dawn, if I settle on the far side of the sea, even there your hand will guide me, your right hand will hold me fast" (Ps. 139:9,10).

There is no point of space, whether inside or outside the bounds of creation, where God is not present. That is why, when we ask the question, "Who's in control?" we can answer without equivocation, *"God is!"*

What Does This Mean to Me?

What does all this have to do with the subject of suffering? Because of His omnipresence and omniscience, God is *with* us in all our struggles and *understands* our trials. Nothing in our lives takes God by surprise. We are not alone in our suffering. We have a God who loves us and is with us in the midst of our problems.

Why Does a Loving God Allow Suffering?

Many people ask, "Why does God allow fear to continue to grip the hearts of men in this enlightened age?" Many are asking, "Where is God's power? Why doesn't He stop all this misery and cruelty with which our age has been cursed?" Others are asking, "How can God be good and merciful, when every day men and women are crushed by agonies almost beyond their endurance?" These questions are asked not only by atheists and enemies of religion, but also by bewildered Christians, who, staggering under the burden of anguish, cry out, "Why must I bear this misery? How can God lay all this suffering on me?"

During the Korean War, I met scores of devout Korean Christians who were asking these same questions, just as they are asking them today in Southeast Asia, Uganda, and scores of other countries.

One of the earliest books in the Bible, the Book of Job, deals with this difficulty. Some today have experienced war, terrorism, broken relationships, financial pressures, and many other hardships. But I doubt they have sustained losses as large as Job's were when treacherous enemies captured his men and all his herds and flocks. Perhaps there is someone whose son or daughter has been held hostage, or who has received notification that his son or daughter was killed in action. Job lost seven sons and three daughters in a single day. Others, perhaps, are stricken by sickness and groaning in pain. Job suffered from some form of sickness that made his body a mass of boils and sores.

When Job could find no human explanation for his afflictions, he cried to God, "tell me what charges you have against me" (Job 10:2).

This age-old question of "Why must the righteous suffer?" is as old as time. There is only one place where we can find an answer and that is in the Bible. Yet in their blindness some men have rejected divine guidance to insist that everything in life comes from chance. *Fate,* they declare, smiles on some people, and they have an easy, untroubled existence. Fate frowns on others, and they are beset with unnumbered difficulties. They say that it is all a matter of luck. "Since we are only creatures of chance," they conclude, "why not press every drop of pleasure out of life while we can, and have our full fling before tomorrow comes and death with it?"

I talked to a school teacher in one of our cities. She said that this same attitude is expressed by some of her students. They say, "We are going to have to go to war anyway, the atomic bomb is going to blow the whole world to smithereens—so why not have a good time now?" What a shocking mistake! And how completely this attitude fails in times of crisis!

Other skeptics have gone to the opposite extreme and declared that men suffer because they are weak. "Learn to be hard and ruthless," they urge. "Smash all opposition. Away with sympathy, kindness and mercy. Down with love. Might makes right. Don't be a weakling—be a superman." That was the delusion of Hitler, and the result was immeasurable misery for millions of people.

Secularists fail to offer satisfying solutions to man's dilemma of suffering. Often humanistic philosophies tend to create further confusion and personal discouragement.

The question of why God allows suffering is one of the most

profound mysteries of life. And it is a difficult question to answer. We cannot turn to any one passage in the Scriptures to find a thorough and conclusive treatment of the subject, but the Bible does hint at some answers. I would like to share with you some ideas which you might find helpful.

First, let us realize that God *has* been active in working toward the alleviation of suffering.

We must remember that suffering originated in the Garden of Eden, as we discussed earlier. God gave man the freedom of choice: to choose good or to choose evil. Part of the human makeup which distinguishes man from other creatures is his ability to reason and make moral decisions. Man is a free moral agent. Satan does *not* give his children that same choice.

Adam chose to follow the advice of Satan, and he rebelled (sinned) against God. Adam's choice (his sin) opened a "Pandora's box" of suffering for mankind. A careful study of Genesis reveals that Adam's action produced a wide spectrum of suffering: physical, spiritual, social, psychological, and even ecological. In a very real sense, the suffering of this world was created by man himself. The tendency to sin, the sinful nature, is a human characteristic transferred from Adam and Eve to the second generation of mankind. And it has been transferred to every generation since. It is part of the human nature we have all inherited.

And yet it is God who took action to solve the problem. In the Garden He gave Adam a ray of hope—the promise that one day He would send His Son (the seed of the woman) to earth to destroy the devil's work and deal with the problems of man's sin and suffering.

We have seen this fulfilled historically in Jesus Christ. By His life, death, and resurrection He triumphed over Satan and sin, and He is the key to the solution of suffering. By His death, He releases us from the penalty of sin. By His resurrection life, He gives us the power over the tendency to sin as we allow Him to control our lives.

Man's sinful actions (murder, theft, rape, terrorism, and so on) inflict suffering upon others. If all men would allow Jesus to reign in their lives, much of this world's suffering would not only be alleviated but abolished.

So we see that God has not been passive regarding man's

plight. He has taken action. In fact, all of history is moving toward a time when Christ will establish His rule over *all* the universe. Satan, sin, and suffering will be eliminated entirely. God promises to free us from the penalty and power of sin; and one day He will produce an environment in which men will be free from the presence of sin and the suffering associated with it. Isaiah 9:6,7: "For to us a child is born, to us a son is given, and the government will be on his shoulders. And he will be called Wonderful Counselor, Mighty God, Everlasting Father, Prince of Peace. Of the increase of his government and peace there will be no end." F. B. Meyer once said, "When our government is upon His shoulder, of its increase and of our peace, there shall be no end."

We must bear in mind that God has acted on our behalf to rid the world of suffering. And the astounding fact is that He did it *by suffering Himself.* He is a Father who witnessed the torture and death of His own Son. God, who loves His Son, allowed Him to suffer so that you and I might be released from suffering. By virtue of Christ's passion and death, those who have accepted Him as their Savior will be freed from the most intense suffering imaginable—eternal separation from God.

It is in God's own suffering that we see His great love. We must not try to evaluate God's character and judge whether or not He is a loving God by looking at our own sufferings. It is by looking at the Cross that we come to know and experience the depth of God's love for us.

Thus we see that God has a plan for the elimination of suffering.

But why doesn't God remove all suffering from our world *now?* He has the power; why doesn't He use it for the good of mankind now?

First, if God were to eradicate *all* evil from this planet, He would have to eradicate all evil men. Who would be exempt? "For all have sinned and fall short of the glory of God" (Rom. 3:23). God would rather *transform* the evil man than eradicate him.

Just the other day we received a letter telling about a prisoner who was sentenced to die in the electric chair. Twenty-four hours before his scheduled execution, it was postponed. However, because of his close brush with death, he came to know God in a personal way through faith in Jesus Christ and has become a vocal witness for Christ there in prison. Of the other prisoners also on death row, twenty-two are now involved in Bible study with him. They were all jolted through his experience—death suddenly became a reality to them—and through his personal relationship with God and witness to that fact, he is being used even there on death row.

In Christ we can become new people. "If anyone is in Christ, he is a new creation; the old has gone, the new has come!" (2 Cor. 5:17). God can produce great good out of any life dedicated to Him.

Second, if God were to remove all evil from our world (but somehow leave man on the planet), it would mean that the essence of "humanness" would be destroyed. Man would become a robot.

Let me explain what I mean by this. If God eliminated evil by programming man to perform only good acts, man would lose his distinguishing mark—the ability to make choices. He would no longer be a free moral agent. He would be reduced to the status of a robot.

Let's take this a step further. Robots do not love. God created man with the capacity to love. Love is based upon one's right to choose to love. We cannot force others to love us. We can make them serve us or obey us. But true love is founded upon one's freedom to choose to respond. Man could be programmed to do good, but the element of love would be lost. If man were forced to do good, suffering would be eliminated—and so would love. What would it be like to live in a world without love?

Thus we can see that God's use of His power to eliminate evil would not prove to be a positive solution to the problem of suffering. The results of such action would create greater dilemmas. Either man would be reduced to the status of a robot in a loveless world or he would be annihilated.

It is really God's love for man which restrains Him from removing evil from our world by a display of His power. God's plan is to remove evil by a display of His love—the love that He demonstrated at Calvary.

It is in God's love that we find the key to the ultimate solution of the problem of suffering. The answer to the age-old question of suffering rests in an understanding and appreciation of the character of God.

This is what Job discovered. At the height of his suffering and questioning, God revealed Himself in various aspects of His character to Job. Job was given an awesome demonstration of God's wisdom. Through this experience he came to realize that God could be trusted on the basis of His character. Although Job could not understand the ultimate purpose for all of God's actions, he could trust God. Because God knows and understands all things, He can be trusted to do what is best.

There will always be secrets and motives of God which lie beyond the grasp of man. God is infinite; man is finite. Our knowledge and understanding are limited. But based upon what we do know about God's character, demonstrated supremely in the Cross, we can trust that God is doing what is best for our lives.

Corrie ten Boom had a good way of explaining the perspective we need when confronting problems in life that puzzle us:

"Picture a piece of embroidery placed between you and God, with the right side up toward God. Man sees the loose, frayed ends; but God sees the pattern."

Who's in Charge?

God is in control. Whatever comes into our lives, no matter how difficult or dangerous it may be, we can confidently say, "We know that in all things God works for the good of those who love him, who have been called according to his purpose" (Rom. 8:28).

*God judged it better to bring good
out of evil than to suffer no evil to
exist.*

ST. AUGUSTINE

4/

*The Birth of a
Suffering World*

MANKIND HAS BEEN plagued since the beginning of time
with a haunting question: "How can a God of love allow the
existence of suffering?" When we see the trouble, tragedy,
and heartache in the world, even sincere believers who
honestly face their own doubts and fears are forced to ask,
"Why, God?"

Through tears or in anger, we hear questions like this:
"Why, God, did you allow this tragedy to occur?" Or, "Why,
God, do you allow this suffering to continue?"

Jack Mowday served in the military as a helicopter pilot. His
wife, Lois, and two of her friends had a special idea about
giving their two husbands and a fiancé a surprise Christmas
gift—a flight in a hot-air balloon. They knew their husbands
had always wanted to ride in the gondola of a hot-air balloon.
So they made the arrangements for December 15, down in
Florida. The day dawned bright and clear.

It was really an exciting moment as the men got into the
gondola. After the balloon lifted off Lois and the members of
the family followed it in two cars. The gondola was floating
low over the housetops, and the husbands, greatly excited,
were singing Christmas carols to the residents down below.
Somehow, in the excitement, they didn't notice the high-

tension wire, and the gondola and balloon caught on it. What had been a moment of joy and triumph turned to tragedy as these women saw their loved ones leap to their death before their eyes. How do a young wife and family cope with something like that?

Speaking at one of our crusades, Lois testified that she knew "that the consuming truth in Jack's mind as he hung from that burning basket on the 15th of December was that when he let go, if he didn't survive his fall, he'd be in heaven with the Lord." She went on to say: "I know tonight, that if I were to die even this very night, that I, too, would be in heaven with the Lord, and with Jack. That total assurance wasn't always there for Jack and me. I was fortunate enough to have transferred my trust from myself to Jesus Christ at the age of 13. And although I didn't have much growth in my Christian life for awhile, I did have the assurance that if anything happened to me, I'd be in heaven.

"Since Jack's death, my own life has changed dramatically. And I think I'd have to say the biggest change has been a really supernatural peace, and an absence of anxiousness. I still worry and have times of apprehension, but in no way like I used to. And I believe that I have this peace because I've been able to see firsthand that the Lord really meets us in our times of need. Although the pain of missing Jack is very real, the comforting presence of the Lord is very real also."

I do not feel adequate to answer questions such as those which I posed at the beginning of this chapter. All I can do is look with you at some of the underlying biblical principles that relate to the origin of evil, which is the root and cause of all suffering since man came into this world. I do know that of God's original creation, the Bible says, without any reservation, "God saw all that he had made, and it was very good" (Gen. 1:31). The process of creation, including man, had been completed, and God looked upon all He had created and pronounced it "good." Total "good" excludes suffering, pain, evil, and tragedy.

Yet only a few verses later, in chapter 3 of Genesis, God said to the man and woman He had created: "I will greatly increase your pains in childbearing; with pain you will give birth to children. . . . Cursed is the ground because of you; through painful toil you will eat of it all the days of your life. It will produce thorns and thistles for you, and . . . By the sweat of your brow you will eat your food until you return to the ground, since from it you were taken; for dust you are and to dust you will return" (Gen. 3:16–19).

Within these verses lies the "seed" of suffering, the prediction of pain and death, both of which have tormented the world ever since. In these words we discover the origin of evil and the cause of man's pains. What had happened between Genesis 1 and 3?

Man's Fall from God's Plan

God's original plan for man was the Garden of Eden—an existence so idyllic one cannot adequately put into words its beauty and richness. Not only was man in a perfect environment, surrounded by natural beauty fresh and unspoiled from the Creator's hand; he also had the privilege of an uninterrupted walk with God, for God's purpose in creating man was to fashion someone with whom He could converse and have fellowship. Indeed, it became God's daily practice to walk with man in the "garden" in the cool of the day (Gen. 3:8).

But man was not content with that arrangement. Rather, he desired to be more like God, to have God's power and knowledge. When Satan in the form of the serpent came to him and asked, "Did God really say, 'You must not eat from any tree in the garden'?" (Gen. 3:1), man succumbed to his temptation to disobey God—and ate of the forbidden tree. This is the event which we call the "Fall" of man—man's direct disobedience to God's command.

It was this direct disobedience that resulted in the judgment God placed on the human race which we quoted from Genesis 3. This is what happened between Genesis 1 and 3—and it was the beginning of all the pain and suffering we know in our world. Christian and non-Christian alike have inherited this imperfection from our common ancestors, Adam and Eve. We call this imperfection "sin"—and sin lies at the heart of chaotic world conditions as we now know them and as they have existed through the centuries.

Let me try to show you how the whole process is going on today.

Revolution in Paradise

The first "world revolution" that succeeded was begun by Satan in the Garden of Eden. God had created a perfect environment, a perfect man, and a perfect woman. However, He gave them freedom of choice. He had to test them. He warned that if they failed the test they would suffer and die, and if they passed the test, God, man, and woman would build a magnificent world through succeeding generations.

Satan was in the garden in the form of a serpent. We can only speculate how this all happened. There are a number of Scriptures that hint as to *who* Satan is, *where* he came from, and *why* he wanted to usurp God's authority and take control of this planet. Very subtly, Satan contradicted God and told Eve, "You will not surely die if you disobey God by eating the forbidden fruit." He further assured them that, if they did eat the fruit, they would be "like God, knowing good and evil." Thus Satan exalted himself above God and endeavored to get mankind to doubt the reliability of God's Word. Beginning in the midst of Edenic bliss, bringing distress and chaos in his wake, he has worked in every conceivable way to thwart, hinder, and defeat the work of God ever since.

The Bible assumes that Adam and Eve were created fully grown. They soon had two sons. Cain, the older, became jealous of Abel, the younger, and killed him. This was the first result of Adam's and Eve's sin being transmitted to their children, and thus it has been transmitted from generation to generation. Since that time, there has always been, just beneath the surface in every heart, the possibility of the worst sins.

Apparently Cain became Satan's first follower after Adam and Eve—his brother Abel a victim. Satan has slaughtered, plundered, and bludgeoned his way through the centuries manifesting himself in every false ideology, sect and cult.

The Crises of History

The next great crisis in human history came several generations later when God looked upon the human race and saw that they were totally corrupt and depraved. He determined to destroy them and start over again. However, there was one godly man whom He would not destroy, and that was Noah. God warned Noah of impending judgment upon the entire world and told him that He was going to save him and his family. God said He was going to destroy the world by a flood, and He instructed Noah to build an "ark" or ship. The Scripture says that "Noah did all that God commanded him." For years he worked on the ship. Finally, when it was finished, God called him, his family, and the animals into the ark. When the flood came, they were saved, and the rest of the human race was destroyed.

Another great crisis came a few generations later. At that time the entire earth was of one language and of one speech (Gen. 11:1). The people were again in revolt against God. They decided to reach *into heaven* by building a tower. They were defiant of God's laws and provisions. The tower was probably a pagan temple designed to tower above everything else in the world. It was really the "religion" of the people. It exalted man instead of God. Again, judgment fell upon the human race. The people could no longer understand each other's speech, and the Bible says the Lord scattered them over all the earth. The name of the place was called Babel. The word *babel* means "to confuse." Thus even the confusion of the languages in the world today and the scattering of people to the various continents was a judgment from God because of man's rebellion.

We see how the seed of sin is transmitted from one generation to another. Today the world is heading for another major crisis that is being called, even by the secular world, "Armageddon."

The Devil's Deception

The devil is aptly named the "father of lies." From the beginning of time he has deceived the gullible men and women of every age.

An old Scottish clergyman said the devil has two lies which he uses at two different stages. Before we commit a sin he tells us that one little sin doesn't matter; it's a trifle, and we can easily recover ourselves again. The second lie is this: after we have sinned he tells us it is hopeless, we are given over to sin and shouldn't attempt to rise. Both are total and terrible lies.

We have all fallen, and God does not consider this a trifle. Judgment hangs over the whole human race because of our fall, which is also defined as rebellion or disobedience. The Scripture says, "Sin entered the world through one man, and death through sin, and in this way death came to all men, because all sinned" (Rom. 5:12). However, because Jesus Christ came and died on the cross and rose from the dead, we are not in a hopeless position. We are in a position to be reconciled to God and put back into a right relationship with Him.

We do not need to believe the devil's lies. Satan is the master of the ultimate double-talk and sophistry. He calls evil good and continues to confuse men with his cleverly disguised untruths.

Man has always been dexterous at confusing evil with good. That was Adam's and Eve's problem, and it is our problem today. If evil were not made to appear attractive, there would be no such thing as temptation. It is in the close similarity between good and evil, right and wrong, that the danger lies.

The Bible says through Isaiah the prophet, "Woe to those who call evil good and good evil, who put darkness for light and light for darkness, who put bitter for sweet and sweet for bitter" (Isa. 5:20).

Today we see social evil, terrorism, and gross immorality throughout the world. Modern social righteousness often differs from the righteousness of the Bible. Someone has said, "A wrong deed is right if the majority of people declare it not to be wrong." By this principle we can see our standards shifting from year to year according to the popular vote! This new permissiveness is condoned by intelligent men and women, many of whom are to be found in the churches.

Divorce was once frowned upon by society and laws against lewdness and obscenity were strictly enforced. But now divorce is accepted, even among church leaders. Fornication, obscenity and lewdness are glorified in much of our literature and films. Perversion is considered a biological abnormality rather than a sin.

These things are contrary to the teaching of God's Word.

And God has not changed. His standards have not been lowered. God still calls immorality a sin and the Bible says God is going to judge it.

It's All Right If—?

I remember when I was a boy on a small farm in North Carolina, a man's word was as good as his bond. I seriously doubt if my father ever signed a contract in the many deals he made for cows, horses, mules, and machinery. A handshake was enough. Today you have to employ lawyers to draw up the most intricate and complex contracts, and even they do not provide a complete safeguard against the fraud, cheating, and lying so prevalent today.

Even a few years ago, honesty was the hallmark of a man of good character. But it's been set aside for an "It's all right if you don't get caught" philosophy. Only when we are in court are we required to tell the truth, the whole truth, and nothing but the truth.

Evil worms its way into our lives by presenting a harmless appearance. What is more beautiful than the full-page, full-color ads of "the man of distinction," dressed impeccably, sipping a glass of whiskey with his friends in the warmth of a well-appointed room? These ads say nothing of the new alcoholics being made every day, nor of the growing problem of alcoholism at the heart of our civilization. Of course it wouldn't be in good taste to show a picture of a "man of distinction" on Skid Row who began his drinking on Fifth Avenue. It wouldn't be in good taste, but it would be honest. "Woe to those who call evil good!"

The young couple, though they have been warned of the psychological, spiritual and even physical dangers of premarital sex, sit in a parked car at a drive-in theater, or rent a motel room for a couple of hours, and flirt with tragedy, all the while calling their present experience "heavenly." That which is heavenly within the framework of true love, the marriage bond, can become a hell of remorse to those who indulge in it outside of marriage. Sometimes our actions lead us into a situation where suffering is inevitable. "Woe to those who call evil good!"

When it comes to social justice and political reform it seems that almost everyone in every group throughout the world is joining in the refrain and shouting for "freedom." Liberation is the new relevant word. I have traveled over much of the world, and I have never found a country where I thought total social justice exists. What people do not realize is that we will never have total social justice in our world until Christ comes back. This is where Marx was wrong. He thought the problem was basically economic, and he was partially right. But the basic problem is the problem of human nature: the greed, jealousy, lust and pride which come from within the heart of man (Mark 7:20–23). Many people today are being misled at this point.

A bishop in a small country worked hard to bring about a social and political revolution in his country. There was no doubt that such a reform was needed. However, he was blind to who his allies were. When the revolution finally took place, he found that his people had jumped from the frying pan into the fire. Within a year after the revolution he stood before a large audience with tears streaming down his cheeks and said, "My God, what have I done! I have misled my people." "Woe to those who call evil good!"

We Want Success Now

How do we get our values so mixed up? How do we fall into this trap of Satan? For one thing, we are shortsighted. We look for shortcuts to happiness. Our lust for immediate pleasure prompts us to think of evil as good.

In one of John Steinbeck's books he has a character saying, "If it succeeds, they will be thought not crooked, but clever." In our desire to achieve success quickly it is easy to get our values mixed up and call evil good and good evil.

We have changed our moral code to fit our behavior instead of changing our behavior to harmonize with God's moral code. Nothing is fixed today. We are not on solid ground. Millions of young people are shifting from one side to the other. They are like unguided missiles filled with energy and ambition and yet somehow not "fitting in." Their elders have led them astray. Peer pressure leads them astray. The undue emphasis on violence, sex, and the debunking of the home on television and films leads them astray. Sometimes the educational system leads them astray intellectually. In thousands of churches they are led astray theologically. Thus spiritually and morally they are drifting aimlessly, without compass or guide.

And yet I find in my travels that most young people really want us to spell out the moral law. They may not accept it or believe it, but they want to hear it, clearly and without compromise.

We tolerate all too easily the false promises of politicians, the misrepresentations in advertising, the cheating in college exams, the exaggerations in conversation, and the everyday dishonesties of Mr. and Mrs. John Doe. We are no longer shocked by the immorality or social injustice going on around us. Even the poorest Americans are richer than the average person in many countries, such as Bangladesh; yet, in comparison with other sections of society, there is poverty in America. Fraud and corruption are being uncovered in many of our social programs for the inner city—the urban problems are mounting by the hour. Racial prejudice is still there, as it was long before the time of Martin Luther King, Jr.

I was riding with a wealthy man in the back seat of his chauffeur-driven Cadillac out to his home on Long Island. We passed along the edge of Harlem. I told him that a few days before I had made a tour of some of the poverty-stricken areas of Harlem and East Harlem. He shrugged his shoulders and said, "That's something we don't think about." If he were a Christian it would be his duty to think about it and do what he could about it. In a true sense we are our brothers' keepers. As Christians we are to be Good Samaritans. But still the basic problem is the human heart.

Who would maintain that the more affluent people of suburbia are basically happier than those of the inner city? Happiness doesn't come from materialism. It comes from the inner peace that we find in our relationship to God.

Man's Self-Centeredness

When something brings profit or pleasure to us, we are inclined to call evil good, even if we know it is dead wrong.

"But it's what I've always wanted," or "I enjoy it, although I know it's wrong" are the alibis we have manufactured to justify evil and call it good.

From self-centeredness to others-centeredness is a contrast we could illustrate from the lives of Pierre and Marie Curie. After discovering the curative powers of radium, they considered the idea of keeping it a secret, having it patented, and getting rich by their discovery. Marie said to Pierre the words which brought them to their decision: "'Physicists always publish their researches completely. If our discovery has a commercial future, that is an accident by which we must not profit. And radium is going to be of use in treating disease. . . . It seems to me impossible to take advantage of that.'"[1]

On the night he died, Pope John Paul I was reading from the classic of Thomas à Kempis, *Imitation of Christ*. The author said, "If thou goest here and there seeking thine own will, thou shalt never be happy or free from care."

What a difference it would make if only we could focus our eyes outward, instead of inward, and heed the words of Jesus, "Seek first his kingdom and his righteousness, and all these things will be given to you as well" (Matt. 6:33).

Many people ask about Christianity the same thing they ask about everything else today: "What's in it for me?" In our selfishness, we think of God as we think of everyone else. What can He contribute to us, personally? In other words, we want God to be our servant. It is this self-seeking spirit which opened the door to Satan in the Garden of Eden and holds the door open to him today.

The Art of Rationalization

We put the blame on someone else, we make excuses for our actions, and we find it easy to call evil good. From Adam, who said, "The woman you put here with me—she gave me some fruit from the tree, and I ate it" (Gen. 3:12), to a congressman who says, "I did nothing that a thousand other men haven't done," we excuse ourselves.

---

1. Eve Curie, *Madame Curie, A Biography,* translated by Vincent Sheean (Garden City, NY: Doubleday, Doran & Co., Inc., 1937), p. 204.

Our Lord was impatient with rationalization. In Luke 18 He told of the self-righteous Pharisee who said, "God, I thank you that I am not like all other men—robbers, evildoers, adulterers—or even like this tax collector" (v.11). The Pharisee kidded himself into thinking he was something, when he was not. But the tax collector, whom the Pharisee looked upon with scorn, saw himself as he was, and said, "God, have mercy on me, a sinner" (v.13). Jesus said, "I tell you that this man, rather than the other, went home justified before God. For everyone who exalts himself will be humbled, and he who humbles himself will be exalted" (Luke 18:14).

How can we get our values right? How can our warped judgment be straightened out? Some tell us that education is the answer to these questions. Prove to people that crime doesn't pay, that illicit sex is psychologically harmful, that excessive drinking is injurious to the body and brain. Programs of social and personal reform are launched continually. Are they the answer to evil?

Others say that science is the answer. Science can make a clean bomb or a harmless cigarette. It can cope with the problems of drugs. Science, they say, can tap the brain of man and alter his desires.

But the Bible, which has withstood the ravages of time, tells us a different story. It says that we are possessed of a sinful, fallen nature which wars against us, that seeks to destroy us. Paul said, "I find this law at work [in me]: When I want to do good, evil is right there with me" (Rom. 7:21). Evil is present to cleverly disguise itself as good. Evil is present to control and deceive us. We are not at peace with ourselves or with God. That is what the Cross of Christ is all about: to reconcile us to God and to give us a new nature.

Man without God is a contradiction, a paradox, a monstrosity. In himself he is totally inadequate. Paul found the cure for his violent, destructive disposition, not at the university, or in the culture of Greece, but on the Damascus road in Syria when he met Jesus Christ. Later he wrote: "Through Christ Jesus the law of the Spirit of life set me free from the law of sin and death" (Rom. 8:2).

Before his conversion Paul saw Christ as the greatest evil, but after he encountered Him, he loved what he had so fervently hated. At last he could see evil as evil, and good as good. "Something like scales fell from Saul's eyes" (Acts 9:18). His values were straightened out, because his nature had been changed by the redeeming grace of God. Despite his conversion, however, Paul did not find freedom from suffering. Christianity is not an insurance policy against life's ills and troubles.

Why Suffering, God?

Why do we suffer? One thing is clear. The Bible insists that there is suffering in the world because there is sin in the world. The heart of the problem lies in man's alienation from God which began with Adam and Eve. If the separation which sin creates had not entered into the life of man, human suffering would not exist in the world.

So another thing is clear. Suffering was not part of God's original plan for man. By willful disobedience to God's Word and commandment, man brought suffering upon himself. He has been reaping what he has sown all through the centuries.

But God has a way of bringing good out of evil, and this is the positive value in suffering.

At the beginning of this chapter we talked about the seeming tragedy in the life of Lois Mowday. As we listen to her story we can have no doubt that God met her in her time of need. As a result, she came to an understanding of the meaning and purpose of suffering in her life.

In the rest of this book I will try to share some of these lessons with you.

He was oppressed and afflicted,
yet he did not open his mouth;
he was led like a lamb to the
slaughter,
and as a sheep before her
shearers is silent,
so he did not open his mouth.
ISAIAH 53:7

5/

The Suffering Savior

NO ONE IN HISTORY ever suffered more than Jesus Christ. The culmination of His suffering came on the cross of Calvary, the supreme symbol of both physical and spiritual suffering.

God's View

We humans view life from our personal point of time and space, but God views us from His heavenly throne in the light of eternity. We see ourselves as self-sufficient, self-important, and self-sustaining; God sees us as dependent, self-centered, and self-deceived. Our worldly wisdom has made us calloused and hard. Our natural wisdom, as the Scriptures teach, comes not from God, but is earthly, sensual, and devilish (James 3:15).

There is a difference between wisdom and knowledge. The fear of the Lord is the beginning of wisdom. All *truth* is from God, whether it be scientific, psychological, philosophic, or religious. The truth in the Bible points us all to the Cross of Jesus Christ. It is there that we find forgiveness of sins and the solution to the dilemmas and problems that face us both corporately and individually.

The wisdom of this world, encouraged by Satan, is cynical of the Cross. The apostle Paul said, "The message of the cross is foolishness to those who are perishing, but to us who are being saved it is the power of God" (1 Cor. 1:18). It is impossible for the "natural man" (the one who does not know Jesus Christ as his personal Savior) to understand how God, in His grace and mercy, can forgive sinners and transform lives. It is also impossible for the natural man to comprehend how these changed lives can affect society. Those with their worldly wisdom do not understand the workings of God. The Bible teaches that the Cross is an "offense" or stumbling block to the unbeliever (1 Cor. 1:23).

When I am on television or in a meeting of any kind, I can preach on almost any subject and most people will accept it. I can speak about social injustice and human suffering and raise money for the poor, refugees or people in distress. But to proclaim Christ crucified is different. Even though the Cross of Christ is the power of God unto salvation, it is also an offense to the world—and always will be. There is a tension here. Though the Cross repels, it also attracts. It possesses a magnetic quality.

Sometime ago I was holding a mission at Cambridge University. I preached on the Cross and experienced, as I always do when dealing with this subject, great freedom and boldness of spirit. Some of the student leaders came to me and asked if I would repeat that sermon two nights later.

I prayed about it, and decided that I would preach another sermon which included a great deal about the blood of Christ. Again I felt tremendous freedom of spirit, and on both occasions the results in dedicated lives at the end of the service were among the greatest of the mission. The Holy Spirit takes the message of the Cross and drives it into the hearts of even the most sophisticated and academic audiences.

The apostle Paul said, "The foolishness of God is wiser than man's wisdom, and the weakness of God is stronger than man's strength" (1 Cor. 1:25).

God's Plan

God says there is no hope for the world aside from the Cross. For centuries the world has rejected God's plan of redemption. Now, because of man's refusal and rebellion, he stands on the threshold of what former Prime Minister Macmillan called "the extinction of civilization itself" (or Armageddon).

Stumbling and fumbling, man thinks that by his own wisdom he can save himself—that somehow he will be able to pull out of this path leading headlong to destruction. God warns that this perverted wisdom of man will lead to judgment.

Glorying in the Cross

The significance of the Cross has been captured by some of our great hymn writers. On a hill overlooking the harbor of Macao, China, Portuguese settlers once built a massive cathedral. But a typhoon proved stronger than the work of man's hands. Some centuries ago the building fell in ruins except for the front wall. High on the top of that wall, challenging the elements down through the years, stands a great bronze cross.

When Sir John Bowring saw it in 1825 he was moved to write those words now so familiar to many:

> In the cross of Christ I glory,
> Towering o'er the wrecks of time:
> All the light of sacred story
> Gathers round its head sublime.

As Easter draws near each year we consider anew the significance of Jesus' death upon the cross. Choirs and congregations across the world sing,

> When I survey the wondrous cross,
> On which the Prince of Glory died,
> My richest gain I count but loss,
> And pour contempt on all my pride.
> Isaac Watts

When Jesus lifted up His voice and cried, "It is finished!" He did not mean that His life was ebbing away or that God's plan had been foiled. Though death was near, He realized that the final obstacle had been overcome and the last enemy had been destroyed. He had fully and triumphantly completed the task of man's redemption.

By His suffering and death on the cross He had removed the last barrier between God and man. With the victorious words, "It is finished!" (John 19:30), He announced that the road from man to God was completed and open to traffic.

Shortly after Jesus had uttered those words, His head fell limp upon His chest. A Roman soldier came and thrust a spear into His side and out came blood and water. Physicians say that a mixture of blood and water indicates that He died of a broken heart. Christ suffered to the uttermost. He poured out the last ounce of His blood to redeem us; He did not spare Himself. His suffering on the cross was complete.

Here was the Son of God dying on a cross which was made for the vilest of sinners. His was the act of substitution raised to the highest degree. Jesus Christ was the Lamb of God who had come to take away the sin of the world by His voluntary suffering and death. Here was the blood of God poured out in selfless love for a dying, hopeless, doomed world.

To many people, the mention of the blood of Christ is distasteful. It grates upon their proud egos to think that such a price had to be paid for their wickedness. A deep revulsion arises within them when we mention the precious blood of Christ and His supreme sacrifice on the cross. To the natural man, as we have already pointed out, Jesus' suffering and death were "foolishness."

The message of the blood, the cross, and the work of redemption is still "foolishness" to a people who would like to believe that man can save himself by his own goodness.

The Dichotomy of Man and God

Modern man is in conflict with the truth of God at this point. *God* speaks of a fall and a condemnation, and His key word is "grace." Modern *man* speaks of the soul's native goodness, its aspirations and natural good will.

Man's key word is "works." *God* speaks of the depths into which men have fallen and the depravity of the natural man. *Man* boasts of his nobility, his ideals, and his progress.

God calls men to believe in Christ or be lost. *Man* says that it is enough to try to be like Christ. Man's goal is imitation, not redemption.

God says that Christ is the Savior of the world. *Man* says that Christ is just a great example.

Slowly we have drifted away from the biblical truth: "Without the shedding of blood there is no forgiveness" (Heb. 9:22). Modern man would like to make of the cross a thing of sentiment—a trinket to be worn around the neck—an ornament on a church steeple or an emblem stamped in gold on our Bibles. A certain romantic interest has gathered around the story of the cross. But it is the suffering and sacrifice of Christ on Calvary that symbolize man's utter helplessness to save himself. The cross as the supreme symbol of suffering reveals two basic facts that cannot be denied: the depth of man's depravity and the immensity of God's love.

I cannot comprehend the efficacy and power of the blood of Christ. There is an element of mystery that cannot be understood with our natural minds. But I do know that all who by faith test its power discover that it can wonderfully change their lives, lift them to a higher plane of living, and bring a satisfaction and fulfillment they have been looking for.

The apostle Peter said that Christians are "chosen according to the foreknowledge of God the Father, by the sanctifying work of the Spirit, for obedience to Jesus Christ and sprinkling by his blood" (1 Pet. 1:2). Peter views trials of faith as essentially productive in the Christian life. To illustrate the point, he refers to the common practice of subjecting gold to such intense heat that the initial form of it is destroyed. Upon remolding, however, the impurities have also perished in the flame. Trials and difficulties may assail the life of a believer, but they also have the ability to remold his character and banish from his life those impurities which might impair growth and service.

A fellow student of mine majored in chemistry while I took my major in anthropology. In his chemistry class he learned how acids act on different substances. In the course of an experiment, the professor gave the class a bit of gold and told them to dissolve it. They left it all night in the strongest acid they had. It failed to dissolve. Then they tried various combinations of acids, but in vain.

Finally, they told the professor they thought gold could not be dissolved. He smiled. "I knew you could not dissolve gold," he said. "None of the acids you have there will attack it, but try this," and he handed them a special bottle of acid. They poured some of its contents into the tube that held the piece of gold; and the gold that had resisted all the other acids quickly disappeared in the royal water. The gold at last had found its master.

The next day in the classroom the professor asked, "Do you know why that acid is called 'royal water'?" "Yes," they replied, "it is because it is the master of gold, a substance which can resist almost anything that can be poured on it."

Then he said, "Fellows, I should take time to tell you that there is another substance just as impervious as gold. It cannot be touched or changed though a hundred attempts are made upon it. That substance is the sinful heart. Trial, affliction, riches, honor, imprisonment, or punishment will not soften or master it. Education and culture will not dissolve or purify it. There is but one element that has power over the sin of the human heart—the blood of Christ, the Savior of the soul."

The blood of Christ is mentioned over and over again in the New Testament. Peter preached it, Paul wrote about it, and the redeemed in heaven sing about it. In a sense, the New Testament is the Book of the Blood.

In Leviticus 17:11 the Scripture says: "The life of a creature is in the blood, and I have given it to you to make atonement for yourselves on the altar; it is the blood that makes atonement for one's life." God taught His people from the very beginning that He could only be approached by the shedding of blood. Blood is ugly and repulsive. Yet blood is symbolic of the taking of life. All the animals slain in the Old Testament times were but types and symbols. They looked forward to the day when the Lamb slain from the foundation of the world would appear in the person of Jesus Christ, who Himself would be slain on the cross and shed His blood for the forgiveness of sins.

We are told that about 400,000 Americans have a heart attack every year. It is really not a heart attack; it is a blood attack. It is the clotting of the blood so that it cannot get to the heart, brain, lungs, or kidneys. Or perhaps a blood clot escapes. It all has to do with the blood. Without the proper flow of blood, we die. Thus blood represents life.

God said that as a result of our rebellion and sin, man must die. Jesus Christ became our substitute. He suffered our death on the cross. Every time we go to church and receive (or see others receive) the bread and wine at Communion we are reminded of the blood that was shed on the cross. When Jesus gave the wine to His disciples at the Last Supper He said, "This is my blood of the covenant, which is poured out for many for the forgiveness of sins" (Matt. 26:28). That blood is essential and indispensable for our salvation. Without its mark upon us, we are unfit to come into the presence of the holy and righteous God.

In the next few pages we'll examine four of the many passages of Scripture which reveal what the blood of Christ can do for us today—Romans 5:9, Hebrews 9:14, 1 Peter 1:18,19, Matthew 26:28.

Acquitted from the Guilt of Sin

First, the blood of Christ justifies and saves us. "Since we have now been justified by his blood, how much more shall we be saved from God's wrath through him!" (Rom. 5:9). The word *justify* comes from the Latin word, *justificare,* which means to account righteous, to clear of guilt, or to acquit.

The word *justification* means "Just-as-if-you-had-never-sinned." It means much more than forgiveness. You and I cannot justify a person who has wronged us. We can only forgive him. God alone can justify.

When Christ was nailed on the cross, that cross was for a notorious criminal named Barabbas. He had long dreaded this day, for it was the day of his execution. But when the authorities came to his cell they came with good news. They said, "Barabbas, you are a fortunate man. Jesus of Nazareth is going to die in your place. We have orders to release you." This criminal was set free. He was absolved of all charges. He was saved from the death he deserved.

This criminal was a type of the human race: rebellious, godless, and heartless. But he was saved by Christ's death. That would have been wonderful even if Barabbas had been the only one saved; but the Bible says, "Since we have now been justified by his blood, how much more shall we be saved from God's wrath through him!" (Rom. 5:9).

An old preacher in England, who had lived on the American prairies in his youth, was involved in street corner evangelism in the small towns and villages. He attracted an audience with his wild-West stories describing how the Indians had saved their wigwams from prairie fires by setting fire to the dry grass adjoining their settlement. "The fire cannot come," he explained, "where the fire has already been. That is why I call you to the Cross of Christ."

He continued his graphic analogy by explaining, "Judgment has already fallen and can never come again!" The one who takes his stand at the Cross is saved forevermore. He can never come into condemnation, for he is standing where the fire has been. The saved person is in God's safety zone, cleansed by the blood of Christ.

Cleansed Consciences and Changed Lives

Second, the blood of Christ cleanses our consciences: "How much more, then, will the blood of Christ, who through the eternal Spirit offered himself unblemished to God, cleanse our consciences from acts that lead to death, so that we may serve the living God!" (Heb. 9:14).

Each of us has a conscience which sits as a judge over our every thought, word, and deed. It speaks with a silent voice, accusing or excusing, condemning or acquitting. It can be sensitive, crude, undeveloped or distorted, depending upon the way we have used or abused it.

The human conscience is defiled by sin, says the Bible. All of us have experienced the backlash of guilt after a transgression. We know the haunting of the heart, the self-reproach of the mind which conscience can bring, the internal suffering that can come from being out of fellowship with God. Sin's effect may be erased from the body, but it leaves its permanent scar on the conscience. Our consciences are seared and defiled by sin.

The conscience of man is often beyond the reach of the psychiatrist. With all of his psychological techniques, he cannot sound its depravity and depth. Man himself is helpless to detach himself from the gnawing guilt of a heart weighed down with the guilt of sin. But where man has failed, God has succeeded. The Bible says that the blood of Christ has power to cleanse the conscience from dead works to serve the living God. This is not mere theory; it is a fact of Christian experience.

From a cleansed conscience emerges a changed life. The alcoholic is able to lift up his head with a new honor, dignity, and self-control. The prostitute is transformed into a modest wife and loving mother. The delinquent, with the youthful lust for evil, finds the peace of Christ and yields his energies to the service of God. The businessman, who knows that some of his transactions have been unethical, is restored to a life of honesty and integrity. The blood of Christ has cleansed their consciences from dead works.

Redeemed by the Blood

Third, we are redeemed by the blood of Christ. The Bible says, "You know that it was not with perishable things such as silver or gold that you were redeemed from the empty way of life handed down to you from your forefathers, but with the precious blood of Christ, a lamb without blemish or defect" (1 Pet. 1:18,19). The word *redeem* means to "buy back"—to recover by paying a price. Not only the first man, but every man since then has plunged headlong into Satan's trap of sin. Man had to be recovered, delivered, and bought back.

The word *redeemed* can be illustrated by the position of a slave who had been captured or enticed into serving one who was not his legal master, but whose real master, intent on recovering the slave's love and service, buys him back at great personal cost. That is what God did for us.

Captured by Satan and enticed into his service, mankind in his disobedience and unfaithfulness did not dismay God nor diminish His love for us. Instead, on the cross, He paid the price for our deliverance, a price unthinkably greater than our true value. He did this because He loved us. We were redeemed, recovered, restored, not with corruptible things of silver and gold, but with the precious blood of Christ (1 Pet. 1:18,19).

A loving mother once saved her little girl from a burning

house, but suffered severe burns on her hands and arms. When the girl grew up, not knowing how her mother's arms became so seared, she was ashamed of the scarred, gnarled hands and always insisted that her mother wear long gloves to cover up that ugliness.

But one day the daughter asked her mother how her hands became so scarred. For the first time the mother told her the story of how she had saved her life with those hands. The daughter wept tears of gratitude and said, "Oh Mother, those are beautiful hands, the most beautiful in the world. Don't ever hide them again."

The blood of Christ may seem to be a grim and repulsive subject to those who do not realize its true significance, but to those who have accepted His redemption and have been set free from the slavery of sin, the blood of Christ is precious. The freed slave never forgets the overwhelming cost of his liberty and freedom.

Have you ever seen a person who was receiving a blood transfusion? The blood was precious, life-giving, and certainly not repulsive.

The blood of Christ purchased the church—that is, the whole company of those who trust in Him for salvation. "Christ loved the church and gave himself up for her" (Eph. 5:25).

When Christ purchased us, He made us a marked people. Upon every heart which embraces the blood of Christ, God places an invisible mark as a token of its redemption.

Have you ever had your hand stamped as you left an amusement park or sports event? The mark itself doesn't show up except when a certain type of light shines upon it. God's light, in the same way, shines upon our hearts to determine who comprises the true church of Christ. Regardless of color, race, or nationality, these blood-marked ones are distinguished as those who have trusted Christ and Him alone for their salvation.

God is the same today as He was of old. When the Israelites were in cruel bondage in Egypt, God delivered them from their slavery. On the evening before their deliverance, every Israelite householder was commanded to kill a lamb and sprinkle the doorpost with the blood. That was a sign to the destroying angel to pass by. God said, "When I see the blood, I will pass over you. No destructive plague will touch you when I strike Egypt" (Exod. 12:13).

There is a legend that on that night of the exodus a young Jewish boy, the firstborn of a family, was so troubled on his sickbed that he could not sleep. "Father," he anxiously inquired, "are you sure that the blood is there?" His father replied that he had ordered it to be sprinkled on the lintel. The restless boy would not be satisfied until his father had taken him up in his arms and carried him to the door to see for himself. But the blood was not there! The order had been neglected! Before midnight the father made haste to put on his door the sacred token of protection.

The blood of the lamb applied over the doorpost on the night of Israel's deliverance from Egypt distinguished the obedient from the disobedient. Just so today the applied blood of the Lamb of God is the distinguishing mark of God's called-out ones, the church.

Charles Haddon Spurgeon commented on Exodus 12:13: God "does not say when *you* see the blood" I will pass over you, "but when *I* see it."[1] My looking to Jesus brings me joy and peace, but it is God's looking to Jesus which secures my salvation.

Christ, our Passover lamb, has been sacrificed for us (1 Cor. 5:7). He suffered supremely on the cross in our place. Just as death came to every home in Egypt on that terrible night, so death is upon every soul not sprinkled with the blood of Christ.

Universal Appeal

Fourth, the blood of Christ was shed for all. When Jesus served the Last Supper to His disciples, He took the cup of wine and said, "This is my blood of the covenant, which is poured out for many for the forgiveness of sins" (Matt. 26:28).

Many of the world's religions appeal to people of a particular race or nationality. One religion makes its appeal

1. Charles Haddon Spurgeon, *The New Park Street Pulpit, Sermons* (Pasadena, Texas: Pilgrim Publications, 1975) p. 31.

mainly to the Arab world. Another religion appeals largely to the Indian mind. Another is slanted toward Oriental philosophy.

But the message of the Cross is good news for the whole of mankind, for everyone who will accept it. In pointing people of every race to Christ, we like John the Baptist cry, "Behold the Lamb of God, which taketh away the sin of the world" (John 1:29, KJV).

Speaking of His crucifixion Jesus Himself said: "I, when I am lifted up from the earth, will draw all men to myself" (John 12:32). By "all men" He did not mean all men without exception, for there are many who refuse to be drawn to Him. He meant rather all men *without distinction,* whether it be of class or color or anything else. His invitation is for Jew and Gentile alike.

The appeal of the Cross of Christ is universal. I have met people of every race and kindred, who have trusted in the merits of Jesus Christ and His shed blood for their salvation. The appeal of the Cross reaches into the opium dens of the Orient, salvaging and redeeming men from a living hell. It touches the hearts of slum dwellers and penthouse owners. It penetrates into the mansions of the elite where men and women live in luxury, bringing a peace and joy which money cannot buy. It changes the headhunter into a soul-saver. It gives men of every nation dynamic and purposeful living.

When a famous financier died some years ago, it was found that the year before his death he had made his will, consisting of about 10,000 words and thirty-seven clauses. The most important clause in his will was his priority in life. He said, "I commit my soul into the hands of my Savior, full of confidence that having redeemed me and washed me with His most precious blood, He will present me faultless before the throne of my heavenly Father. I entreat my children to maintain and defend at all hazards, and at all costs personally, the blessed doctrine of the complete atonement of sin through the blood of Jesus Christ once offered, and through that alone."

This man knew his vast wealth was as powerless as the beggar's poverty to bring him salvation. In this he was as dependent as the dying thief at Calvary, dependent upon the mercy of God and the shed blood of Christ just as every one of us is, no matter what our situation in life may be.

Christ Crucified—an Example of Suffering

The New Testament, while insisting that the true purpose for which Jesus suffered was to deal with our sins, also points us to the suffering Savior as a pattern of how we, as His believing people, should endure *our* sufferings.

Thus the apostle Peter, when addressing Christian slaves, urges them to bear their sufferings submissively, even though they have done no wrong: "To this you were called, because Christ suffered for you, leaving you an example, that you should follow in his steps. 'He committed no sin, and no deceit was found in his mouth.' When they hurled their insults at him, he did not retaliate; when he suffered, he made no threats. Instead, he entrusted himself to him who judges justly" (1 Pet. 2:21–23).

Christ has left us an *example*. The Greek word used for *example* is derived from school life and refers to a pattern of writing to be copied by the child learning to write. Christ is our copybook. We look at Him and learn how suffering is to be borne.

In the passage the apostle draws attention to four things about the suffering Savior. First, His holy life: "He committed no sin"; second, His guileless speech: "no deceit was found in his mouth"; third, His patient spirit: "When they hurled their insults at him, he did not retaliate; when he suffered, he made no threats"; and fourth, His implicit faith: "he entrusted himself to him who judges justly."

The writer to the Hebrews also urges his readers, who were being persecuted for their faith, to remember Christ's example of suffering. He writes: "Let us fix our eyes on Jesus, the author and perfecter of our faith, who for the joy set before him endured the cross, scorning its shame, and sat down at the right hand of the throne of God." Then he adds, "Consider him who endured such opposition from sinful men, so that you will not grow weary and lose heart" (Heb. 12:2,3).

Yes, *consider Him.* In our sufferings and tribulations Jesus Himself must be our chief consideration. We must fix our eyes upon Him. He who suffered for us shows us how we are to bear our sufferings.

Men and women have lightly made of the cross a piece of

jewelry, but for God it was the supreme sacrifice He had to make for man's disobedience. Just as suffering came into the world because of one man's (Adam's) disobedience, so release from that suffering came as a result of one Man's (Christ's) obedience. As Paul puts it in Romans 5:19, "For just as through the disobedience of the one man the many were made sinners, so also through the obedience of the one man the many will be made righteous." The power of sin has been broken by the all-sufficient sacrifice of Christ on Calvary, and completely overcome by His victorious resurrection on the Sunday morning we call Easter. That is why we can sing with the hymn writer:

In the cross of Christ I glory!

> *Daddy later developed rheumatoid arthritis. . . . He was never without pain, except when asleep, for the last ten years of his life. I believe his attitude through all the suffering gave credibility to his Christian witness.*[1]
>
> ALLAN EMERY

6/

Why Aren't Christians Exempt?

WE HAVE A HUMAN tendency to wonder why the person who loves God and tries to live an exemplary Christian life has to suffer physically, psychologically, or in any other way, during his time on earth.

The suffering of believers has baffled Jews and Christians since the earliest days. Job is the classic example of a suffering believer. There was an extremely important reason for his suffering. But Job did not know it while he was going through it. Job did not even have the Book of Job to comfort him as we do! Daniel was placed in the lions' den; Shadrach, Meshach, and Abednego were bound and thrown into a fiery furnace; Joseph was cast into prison; Moses had to flee from Egypt and live away from everything he had known for forty years. The reason for all these things was not known at the time. It had to be seen in retrospect. None of us will ever know the full meaning of why believers suffer until we get to heaven.

If our believing forefathers were not exempt, why should we be?

The quote at the beginning of this chapter is from a book by my longtime friend, Allan Emery, Jr. He is a man gifted with

---

1. Allan Emery, *A Turtle on a Fencepost* (Waco: Word Books, 1979), p. 85.

rare spiritual insights, along with a great sense of humor. His spiritual acumen is largely the result of his family heritage. Both of his parents were quiet, courageous Christians who openly shared and lived their faith before their children. Both are recognized by Allan in his book as shapers of his own spiritual stance. Interestingly enough, in common with many Christians, his parents suffered severely in their old age, and both witnessed winsomely, uncomplainingly, gloriously, and faithfully for Christ in and through their physical suffering, as Allan recounts with deep affection.

Spokesmen for God

The apostle Peter wrote a great deal about suffering Christians. He knew, as did most of the early followers of Jesus, what it meant to suffer for his faith. Tradition tells us he died hanging upside down on a Roman cross, because he felt unworthy to die in the same way as his master. Peter suffered in many other ways, both physical and mental, during his walk with the Lord, but throughout his writings the positive value of suffering is emphasized. As he develops this subject, he echoes the words of his Savior as recorded in the Gospels, and of his fellow apostles.

How Mary, the most blessed of all women, and the mother of Jesus, must have suffered! Imagine the insults of friends, who thought she was immoral. Or, years later, her suffering during the humiliations of Jesus culminating on the cross. Standing at the foot of the cross she saw her Son die one of the most agonizing and shameful deaths man ever devised. In the eyes of the people about her, He was a common criminal. She heard the jeering. She saw the soldier thrust the spear in His side.

Yet she believed God. She could not forget the visit of the angel who had told her, "You . . . are highly favored! The Lord is with you. . . . Do not be afraid, Mary, you have found favor with God. You will be with child and give birth to a son, and you are to give him the name Jesus. He will be great and will be called the Son of the Most High. The Lord God will give him the throne of his father David, and he will reign over the house of Jacob forever; his kingdom will never end" (Luke 1:28–33).

As she witnessed the seeming tragedy of the crucifixion, Mary must have asked herself, "Could I have been mistaken? Did I have a false vision? Is He really to be the King who shall rule forever?"

Being human, she must have questioned the past in the light of the incredible suffering of the present on the part of one she loved so much. At the time she was incapable of fully realizing this was the fulfillment of prophecy. If the human race was to have any possibility of reconciliation with God, her Son had to die in this precise way as the prophets had predicted.

Christians Suffer Because They Are Human

We can get a few glimpses here and there in the Scriptures as to why believers are not exempt from suffering. We are also given some definite reasons.

First, Christians suffer because they're human. The fact that we are Christians doesn't mean we are exempt from illnesses, heartaches, natural disasters, tragedies, and ultimately death. Of course, we hear of Christians who have been miraculously delivered or healed. Equally, we hear of others who go through the fires of affliction as, for example, Paul did with his "thorn in the flesh." But it is not all mystery. We hear the Lord saying to Paul in effect: "There's a reason for this thorn in the flesh. It is so you will not be exalted above measure. But you will find that my grace is sufficient to enable you to endure it."

Some years ago I conducted a memorial service for those who had died in tornadoes which almost destroyed a Texas town. Christians died and were injured along with the non-Christians.

Thus, Christians are not exempt from disasters, troubles, and illness. These things are the common lot of mankind and we are involved in them because we share the human experience, just as Christ did.

Often Christians Suffer Because They Deserve It

Second, Christians are not exempt from suffering when they sin and disobey God. If a Christian loses his temper, tells a lie, or commits a sin of any kind, he will suffer God's chastisement or "judgment" (see 1 Cor. 11:28–32; 1 Pet. 4:17–19). Just as a child needs correcting, so God's children need correcting. The Scripture says, "My son, do not make light of the Lord's discipline, and do not lose heart when he rebukes you, because the Lord disciplines those he loves, and he punishes everyone he accepts as a son. Endure hardship as discipline; God is treating you as sons. For what son is not disciplined by his father? . . . No discipline seems pleasant at the time, but painful. Later on, however, it produces a harvest of righteousness and peace for those who have been trained by it" (Heb. 12:5–11).

If, through carelessness or indifference, we ignore traffic laws, we deserve to be arrested and punished like anyone else. If we are unloving or unfaithful in our Christian life, we will pay for it with a guilty conscience or chastisement from God.

A Christian has tremendous responsibilities to his own family. He or she has a responsibility of loving each member of the family. Husbands and wives are to love each other, and submit to one another. We are to train our children in the way in which they should go. If we neglect these responsibilities we will suffer the consequences—perhaps not immediately, but later on.

I know of a Christian leader. He has been unkind to his wife for years, and she suffered a complete physical and mental breakdown. Now he is infatuated with his secretary. He wants to remain a Christian leader in his community, but he cannot have his cake and eat it, too. He is suffering a horrible battle within his own soul. The smile has left his face, the joy has left his heart. His situation is now so obvious that other Christians, knowing the circumstances, are not only praying for him but unfortunately exposing his sin. His suffering is almost unbearable—all because of his own sin—but as yet he has not repented.

There Is No Christian Fallout Shelter

Third, there is no Christian "fallout shelter." Christians are not exempt from suffering, because if they were, non-Christians would beat a path to the church door as though it were a fallout shelter. Again, in recent years we have seen some embrace Christianity, especially in America, because it seemed the smart thing to do.

The popularity of evangelical Christianity has grown in the United States and other countries in the past few years. Many non-Christians feel that for business or political reasons they should belong to the church and make a Christian profession which is not backed up by their lives. Consequently the church in America has been deeply infiltrated by the "world," and in the process it is beginning to copy and resemble the world in many of its activities.

As in Christ's day, there are hypocrites in the church—even in the pulpit or teaching in Bible schools and seminaries. Jesus said, "Woe to you . . . hypocrites! because you shut the kingdom of heaven in men's faces; for you neither enter yourselves, nor do you allow those who are about to go in to do so" (Matt. 23:13, AMPLIFIED). Many Christians who profess Christ do not live as though they possess Him.

However, as we may be approaching events leading to the "last days," the true and the false will start sifting out. When suffering and persecution come upon us there will be a difference. Certainly, when we all stand before the judgment seat of Christ, we will have our true motives revealed.

God Uses Suffering and Trials to Discipline Us

Fourth, God uses suffering and trials to discipline us. Jesus says in Revelation 3:19, "Those whom I love I rebuke and discipline." Our Christian life, if we are to become what God wants us to be, must be one of faith plus suffering. God has His divine plan for shaping our lives, and that plan often includes suffering. The fire of chastening purifies our lives and deepens our spirit. If our Savior was made "perfect through suffering" (Heb. 2:10), how can we expect to escape?

Have you ever considered that steel is iron plus fire; soil is rock plus crushing; linen is flax plus the comb that separates, and the flail that pounds, and the shuttle that weaves!

When I talk about suffering, which includes all the elements of pain and anguish known to man, not just physical pain, I am no different from you. I would have liked to lead a life free of problems, free of pain, free of severe personal discipline; but I have had pressures in my life until I have wanted to "flee"—or been tempted to ask the Lord to take me to heaven. As C. S. Lewis put it in *The Problem of Pain:* "You would like to know how I behave when I am experiencing pain, not writing books about it. You need not guess, for I will tell you; I am a great coward. . . . But what is the good of telling you about my feelings? You know them already: they are the same as yours. I am not arguing that pain is not painful. Pain hurts."[2]

If God loves us so much, why does He allow such things as cancer, tumors, or innumerable sicknesses and diseases?

As I am rewriting this chapter, word has reached me that the wife of one of my friends in Australia has an inoperable malignant tumor of the brain. I have also just received word that the wife of one of my dearest friends, who is a well-known evangelist, has a malignancy.

Many times we are tempted to ask: why?

Sometime ago we heard of a woman missionary who had been raped by bandits. Her husband was shot and killed in the yard in front of their house. She sat for two days with her little children, afraid to move for fear the bandits might return. Then she had to go out and bury her husband.

When my wife heard this story she was deeply troubled for three days. She studied the Scriptures. She asked herself: "Lord, where were the promises?" Then she came to Hebrews 11 and there is a list of the great heroes of the faith. Many of them were gloriously and wonderfully delivered because of their faith.

They were people "who through faith conquered kingdoms, administered justice, and gained what was promised; who shut the mouths of lions, quenched the fury of the flames, and escaped the edge of the sword; whose weakness was turned to strength; and who became powerful in battle and routed foreign armies. Women received back their dead, raised to life again" (Heb. 11:33–35).

But wait. Did all of those early believers escape trials? No. In the middle of the thirty-fifth verse comes a dramatic and

---

2. (New York: The Macmillan Co., 1955), p. 93.

drastic change. It says: *"Others* were tortured and refused to be released, so that they might gain a better resurrection. Some faced jeers and flogging, while still others were chained and put in prison. They were stoned; they were sawed in two; they were put to death by the sword. They went about in sheepskins and goatskins, destitute, persecuted and mistreated—the world was not worthy of them. They wandered in deserts and mountains, and in caves and holes in the ground" (vv.35–38, italics mine).

Some were delivered, and some were not delivered, according to "the will and plan of God." Here we have God's "Medal of Honor" Society. Why were those others not delivered? The last two verses of Hebrews 11 tells us: "And all of these, though they won divine approval by [means of] their faith, did not receive the fulfillment of what was promised. Because God had us in mind *and* had something better *and* greater in view for us, so that they [these heroes and heroines of faith] should not come to perfection apart from us, [that is, before we could join them]" (vv.39,40, AMPLIFIED). In other words, the Scripture says that God has something better for them. The Scriptures indicate that their rewards may even be greater in the future life because they suffered when there was no relief in sight. They believed and trusted even when they were not delivered. We need to realize that when God allows these things to happen, there is a reason which will eventually be known to the individual—most likely not till we get to heaven.

Profit from Discipline

Fifth, there is a profit from discipline. As we have already seen, Job underwent every test Satan could devise, with God's permission. As a result, Job came out of the testing fire "as gold," with all waste refined away and only the purest metal remaining. It may be difficult to understand why a test comes our way, but we must never forget that the test is accomplishing refining and purification. The apostle Peter tells his readers the reason for their trials and persecutions: "These have come so that your faith—of greater worth than gold, which perishes even though refined by fire—may be proved genuine and may result in praise, glory and honor when Jesus Christ is revealed" (1 Pet. 1:7).

We can determine to profit from the experience of suffering, bearing it patiently and learning from it, rather than fighting it.

This is what Job concluded: "When he has tested me, I will come forth as gold" (Job 23:10). That is reacting positively to testing, building on it, rather than criticizing it for interfering with life's normal pattern.

Some of the most beautiful flowers I have ever seen have been artificial, made of silk, plastic, or wax. Interestingly, however, they never attract the bugs. It is the live flowers that attract them.

Christians automatically attract demons, who are constantly harassing, disturbing, and attempting to destroy.

But God uses this for a purpose also. The trials that often come into a Christian's life are the fulfillment of God's gracious purpose as He seeks to build up His child in the most precious faith, developing in His loved one the Christlike spirit that leads to joy and "gold."

Dr. Faris D. Whitesell says: "Physical sufferers, rightly oriented with God, learn some things that others miss. They come to a more correct evaluation of what is really worthwhile in life, their spirits are chastened, their motives are purified, their sympathies are deepened, and their characters are sweetened."

Have you ever looked at a priceless painting and wondered what gave it its value? Looking at a Rembrandt, I realize that he used a canvas and paints, just as other artists, and yet his paintings are invaluable works of art. The difference is the artist himself. God is the artist of our lives, using the strokes of His brush to create a thing of beauty. But our painting is incomplete. God has not finished with us yet.

Dr. M. R. DeHaan gave us a descriptive analogy of this principle. "It is said that a bar of steel worth $5 when made into ordinary horseshoes will be worth only $10. If this same $5 bar is manufactured into needles, the value rises to $350, but if it is made into delicate springs for expensive watches, it will be worth $250,000. This original bar of steel is made more valuable by being cut to its proper size, passed through the heat again and again, hammered and manipulated, beaten and pounded, finished and polished, until it is finally ready for its delicate task."[3]

In these days of inflation the price would be far more than the figures Dr. DeHaan used years ago. However, it illustrates the truth that God's discipline and chastening builds Christian character; and that is one of the reasons why we are not exempt from the problems and difficulties of life.

Many Christians, when being disciplined by God, fall back into self-pity and bitterness. They find their lives buried under the debris of depression. Our difficulties should be stepping stones. Our witness, then, will be like that of "Daddy" Emery, with which we opened this chapter. The choice is ours; the power is God's!

To Keep Us Humble and on Our Knees

Sixth, God allows the fires of tribulation to come into our lives in order to make us, and keep us, humble. He could have delivered Paul from that "thorn in the flesh," but He refused all of Paul's requests for relief and instead promised His grace.

God also does not exempt Christians from suffering because it deepens their prayer life. Nothing will drive us to our knees quicker than trouble. Sometimes in our prayers we wonder why the answer is delayed or does not seem to come at all. Many of God's sufferers are praying for relief, but God's answer seems to be "No." Healing may not come, but God does answer our prayers. He does not always answer them in the way we want. We may not have prayed according to the will of God. In the Garden of Gethsemane as Jesus faced the Cross He prayed: "Father, *if thou be willing,* remove this cup from me" (Luke 22:42, KJV, italics mine). Our prayers must be in accordance with the will of God for the simple reason that God knows better what is good for us than we know ourselves.

Without the experience of suffering or affliction of some kind, we would never become the prayer warriors we should

---

3. *Broken Things* (Grand Rapids: Zondervan, 1948), p. 51.

be. On the natural level we tend to neglect the privilege of prayer until we encounter suffering or difficulty of some kind. We often need to be driven to real prayer by the circumstances that surround us.

Dwight L. Moody was fond of pointing out that there are three kinds of faith in Jesus Christ: *struggling faith,* which is like a man floundering and fearful in deep water; *clinging faith,* which is like a man hanging to the side of a boat; and *resting faith,* which finds a man safe inside the boat—strong and secure enough to reach out his hand to help someone else.

That is the sort of faith you and I have to acquire in order to be effective as Christians—and such faith may be ours through the ministry of suffering in our lives.

George Matheson, who found he was going blind at the age of eighteen, overcame his handicap and became one of the finest scholars and preachers of the Scottish Church. He wrote: "Thou, O Lord, canst transform my thorn into a flower. And I want my thorn transformed into a flower. Job got the sunshine after the rain, but has the rain been all waste? Job wants to know, and I want to know, if the shower had nothing to do with the shining. And Thou canst tell me—Thy Cross can tell me. Thou hast crowned Thy sorrow. Be this my crown, O Lord. I only triumph in Thee when I have learned the radiance of the rain."

To Teach Us Patience

Seventh, suffering also teaches us patience. These words were found penned on the wall of a prison cell in Europe: "I believe in the sun even when it is not shining. I believe in love even when I don't feel it. I believe in God even when He is silent."

Sometimes God seems so quiet! However, when we see the way He works in lives imprisoned by walls or circumstances, when we hear how faith can shine through uncertainty, we begin to catch a glimpse of the fruit of patience that can grow out of the experience of suffering.

Peter says, "How is it to your credit if you receive a beating for doing wrong and endure it? But if you suffer for doing good and you endure it, this is commendable before God" (1 Pet. 2:20).

People suffer some misfortune and ask God for an explanation in the light of His many promises. They often quote one of my favorite verses, Romans 8:28, "We know that in all things God works for the good of those who love him, who have been called according to his purpose." Christians will ask, "How can this work together for my good?" Only God can make it work for good, and He can't do it unless we cooperate with Him. In all of our praying we must ask that His will may be done.

I heard about a man near my home who was going to buy a cow. He was a Christian, and as he passed some fellow Christians on the way he told them that his purpose was to go and buy a cow from a neighbor a mile away. His Christian friends suggested that he should say, "If it be God's will, I am going to buy a cow." He said, "No, I've got the money in my pocket, and I'm going to buy the cow." About an hour later he returned along the same road. He was bloody, bruised, and his clothes were torn. He had been set upon by some robbers who happened to know he had money in his pocket. His friends asked him, "Where are you going now?" He said, "I am going home, *if the Lord wills.*"

By what he suffered that man had been taught a great lesson which all of us should learn. God is in control of events, and we must be patient and submissive to His will.

I take several newspapers at my home every day, both from England and the United States. As I glance through them or watch the television news, I am aware of the terrible suffering, terrorism, crime and injustice that exist in our world and I sometimes cannot help but ask the question "Why?" As the nations of the world are arming as never before in history, as Armageddon looms nearer, it is a comforting thought to know that God is behind everything which touches my life. Things happen to me that I cannot understand, but I never doubt God's love. In the hour of trial I may not be able to see His design, but I am confident it must be in line with His purpose of love.

I may not know His plans, but I know He knows, and that's enough for me.

Elie Wiesel, one of the best known Jewish writers, went through Auschwitz and wrote, "Heaven is the place where questions and answers become one."

My wife, Ruth, once wrote:

> I lay my "whys"
> before Your Cross
> in worship kneeling,
> my mind too numb
> for thought,
> my heart beyond
> all feeling.
>
> And worshiping,
> realize that I
> in knowing You
> don't need a "why."[4]

Ours may be the heritage of the withheld promises. We have been blessed through the endurance and faithfulness of those who have suffered in the past; and people around us, or those who will succeed us, may be blessed through our trials and sufferings and how we react to them.

But we will not know the total answer till we get to heaven. Jesus said, "In that day you will no longer ask me anything" (John 16:23). When we look back and see all the factors involved, we will say it was according to plan.

---

4. Ruth Bell Graham, *Sitting by My Laughing Fire* (Waco: Word Books, 1977), p.88.

In this world you will have trouble. But take heart! I have overcome the world.
JESUS CHRIST (JOHN 16:33)

7/

Suffering Predicted

IN SOME CHURCHES today and on some religious television programs, we see the attempt to make Christianity popular and pleasant. We have taken the cross away and substituted cushions.

As we have already seen, we do not find in the New Testament any indication that Christians should expect to be popular, comfortable, and successful in this present age. Jesus said: "If the world hates you, keep in mind that it hated me first. If you belonged to the world, it would love you as its own. As it is, you do not belong to the world, but I have chosen you out of the world. That is why the world hates you. Remember the words I spoke to you: 'No servant is greater than his master.' If they persecuted me, they will persecute you also. If they obeyed my teaching, they will obey yours also" (John 15:18–20).

Thus Christ said the world system dominated by evil hated Him, and He predicted that it would hate us too.

This age is interested in medals, but not in scars. We can identify with James and John who wanted choice seats in the kingdom. We might even ask for reclining chairs and soft music. But Christ answered His disciples and said that He was not offering seats of honor, but suffering.

Look at our Lord. He was despised and rejected of men. He

was ridiculed, insulted, persecuted, and eventually killed. In the face of opposition He went about "doing good." Even His enemies could find no fault in Him. He became the greatest teacher of morality the world has ever known. However, after three years of public ministry He died an outcast. How quickly the world turned on Him, proving the Scripture that "men loved darkness . . . because their deeds were evil" (John 3:19).

A "good" man is usually a rebuke to the world. As I said earlier, the Bible lists in Hebrews 11 the heroes of the faith, both Jew and Gentile, who were tortured, imprisoned, stoned, torn asunder, tempted, slain with the sword. They went about in sheepskins and goatskins, destitute, afflicted, tormented. These early believers wandered in deserts, in mountains, and hid in caves. That was what it meant to be one of God's people.

As we watch the television specials of Bible stories from the comfort of our living rooms in countries like America, we are grateful that it's easier and more acceptable to be a Christian today. But that will change. In countries like ours we have been living through an abnormal period. It is much more normal for the Christian to be rebuked, criticized and persecuted than to be popular. Great crowds followed our Lord in the earlier part of His ministry as He healed the sick, raised the dead, and fed the hungry. However, the moment He started talking about the cross and the necessity of His death, and telling His followers that they too must take up their cross, "many . . . no longer followed him" (John 6:66). When He spelled out the cost of discipleship it eliminated many of His followers.

In many parts of the world it still means suffering to become a true believer. You may be torn away from your family, home, and friends. You may become a "spectacle" to the world. Suffering has many forms. You may be like the blind man of John 9, unwittingly and unknowingly suffering for the ultimate glory of God.

Many forms of suffering are predicted in the Bible. The following is a list by Dr. Finis Dake:[1]

---

1. *Dake's Annotated Reference Bible, The New Testament* (Grand Rapids: Zondervan, 1961), p. 270.

1. Persecutions for righteousness
   (Matt. 5:10; 13:21; Mark 10:30; John 15:20)
2. Revilings and slander
   (Matt. 5:11–12; 10:25; Acts 13:45; 1 Pet. 4:4)
3. False accusations
   (Matt. 10:17–20)
4. Scourgings for Christ
   (Matt. 10:17)
5. Rejection by men
   (Matt. 10:14)
6. Hatred by the world
   (Matt. 10:22; John 15:18–21)
7. Hatred by relatives
   (Matt. 10:21–36)
8. Martyrdoms
   (Matt. 10:28; Acts 7:58)
9. Temptations
   (Luke 8:13; James 1:2–16)
10. Shame for His name
    (Acts 5:41)
11. Imprisonments
    (Acts 4:3; 5:18; 12:4)
12. Tribulations
    (Acts 14:22; 2 Thess. 1:4)
13. Stonings
    (Acts 14:19; 2 Cor. 11:25)
14. Beatings
    (Acts 16:23; 2 Cor. 11:24–25)
15. Being a spectacle to men
    (1 Cor. 4:9)

The word *spectacle* comes from the same Greek word from which we get the word *theater*. We demonstrate to men and angels the sufferings of Christ as on a stage.

We are fools for Christ's sake (1 Cor. 4:10). The word *fools* comes from a Greek word that carries with it the idea of moronic. It also refers to the hisses, hooting, mockery, and other insults flung at those on the stage of the arena.

16. Misunderstandings, necessities, defamation, and despisings
    (1 Cor. 4:10–13)
17. Troubles, afflictions, distresses, tumults, labours, watchings, fastings, and evil reports
    (2 Cor. 6:8–10; 11:26–28)

18. Reproaches
    (Heb. 13:13; 1 Pet. 4:14)
19. Trials
    (1 Pet. 1:7; 4:12)
20. Satanic opposition
    (Eph. 4:27; 6:12)

But the Bible also teaches that there will be tremendous rewards for those who endure suffering for the name of Christ. Dake lists:[2]

1. Greater glory in heaven
   (2 Cor. 4:17) . . .
3. Making Jesus known
   (2 Cor. 4:11)
4. [Bringing] life to others
   (2 Cor. 4:12)
5. Making grace manifest
   (2 Cor. 4:15) . . .
7. [Reigning] with Christ
   (2 Tim. 2:12) . . .
9. [Giving] glory to God
   (1 Pet. 4:16)
10. [Experiencing] great joy
    (1 Pet. 4:13–14)

In countries like America, people are not necessarily called upon to endure physical suffering because they are believers. However, there are many other types of suffering.

What about the average professing Christian? Living for the Lord Jesus Christ does not seem to be a priority. Sometimes it is difficult to differentiate the Christian from the man of the world. In America, for example, churchgoing has become popular, but churchgoing may not necessarily be accompanied by genuine depth in prayer and Bible study or a change in life style.

The Scripture says, "If anyone is in Christ, he is a new creation; the old has gone, the new has come!" (2 Cor. 5:17).

---

2. Ibid.

Those who believe are expected to be different from the world about them. They are to be members of the new society and the new community that God has created.

Many sit in comfortable pews and sing without thinking,

> Our fathers, chained in prisons dark,
> Were still in heart and conscience free:
> How sweet would be their children's fate,
> If they, like them, could die for thee.
> Frederick W. Faber

Paul told Timothy, "Everyone who wants to live a godly life in Christ Jesus will be persecuted [will suffer]" (2 Tim. 3:12).

Jesus invited us not to a picnic, but to a pilgrimage; not to a frolic, but to a fight. He offered us, not an excursion, but an execution. Our Savior said that we would have to be ready to die to self, sin, and the world. He challenged us to take up a cross, and said that in the world we would have tribulation.

Too many Christian TV and radio programs have been geared to please, entertain, and gain the favor of this world. The temptation is to compromise, to make the gospel more appealing and attractive. At times in the crusades we have conducted, I have looked into the cameras and realized that several million people were watching me. I know that many of the things I have said from the Scriptures have offended, and I have sometimes been tempted to tone down the message. But, God helping me, I never will! I would become a false prophet. I would also betray my Lord. The price of serving Christ is not cheap.

Too many times we are concerned with how *much,* instead of how *little,* like this age we can become. We try to argue that the times are better, that humanity is more Christian, and that the church is in better standing, so that we need not suffer as our forefathers did. We want to be relevant—"one of the boys" at the club, or "one of the girls" at the bridge game. However, the more relevant we become to a sin-dominated world, the more irrelevant we actually are to God, without realizing it.

In Romans 12:2 Paul writes: "Do not conform any longer to the pattern of this world, but be transformed by the renewing of your mind." J. B. Phillips has a striking rendering of these words: "Don't let the world around you squeeze you into its own mold, but let God remold your minds from within."

It's very easy for Christians to allow themselves to be squeezed into the world's mold. Often they are under the illusion that by not being "different," they are making themselves more acceptable to their non-Christian friends. But this is a big mistake. The world doesn't really have much respect for Christians who adopt its fashions and ideas. It is inclined to regard them with contempt—to write them off either as cowards who are ashamed of their faith or as frauds whose profession is not sincere.

Our job in life is not to be popular, but to be faithful. It's more important to have the Master's "Well done" than the world's "Hail, fellow, well met." It's better to be thought of as a man of God than as a man of the world. The Bible says, "Don't you know that friendship with the world is hatred toward God? Anyone who chooses to be a friend of the world becomes an enemy of God" (James 4:4).

Counting the Cost

Salvation is free, but discipleship costs. Two thousand years before Christ, Moses had to choose between the reproach of God and the pleasures of Egypt. The rich young ruler had enjoyed luxury and plenty. He wasn't interested in suffering or sacrifice any more than we are. He probably could have been a member of the average church today. But before a man could join a church in those early days, Christ made him count the cost. In John 6 we read that when great multitudes went after Him, He told them three times that unless they were willing to pay the price, they could not be His followers.

It is never said, "Christ *and*. . . ," it is always "Christ *or* . . . ." Christ *or* Belial, Christ *or* Caesar, Christ *or* the world, Christ *or* Antichrist. Jesus said, "He who is not with me is against me, and he who does not gather with me scatters" (Matt. 12:30).

We have made Christianity too easy, especially in some parts of the world where Christianity is in the majority. In the early days, as in most of the world today, the followers of

Jesus had to count the cost. They had to be willing to deny themselves, pick up their cross, and follow Jesus. But today, particularly in some Western countries, we do not make such demands upon our church members. The church has lost its ability to discipline members who live openly in sin. Consequently, we have lost our witness in the community.

Branded with the Marks of Christ or the Devil

Those of us who profess to be Christians need to ask ourselves: "Do we bear the marks of Christ?" or "Do we bear the marks of whatever enslaves us?" The slave is always branded by his master. This hedonistic generation advertises itself by dissipated faces, trembling hands, and jittery behavior. All the sedatives cannot quiet them, nor can cosmetics hide the scars. They bear the marks of their master.

Many times I have stood on a street corner and read the faces of the people who passed by. Sometimes I could see the marks of a vicious temper, hidden resentments or evil thoughts; they show in the wrinkles, the droop of the mouth, the look in the eyes.

The Bible teaches that no one can serve (be a slave of) two masters. The devil has his slaves, and Christ has His. You and I are either branded with the marks of Christ or with the marks of the devil. The Bible says that some of the marks of the devil are "Adultery, fornication, uncleanness, lasciviousness, Idolatry, witchcraft, hatred, variance, . . . wrath, strife, seditions, heresies, Envyings, murders, drunkenness, revellings, and such like." Furthermore, those who indulge in "such things shall not inherit the kingdom of God" (Gal. 5:19–21, KJV).

The Christian Bears Scars Too

We Christians are to bear the marks of *our* master just as noticeably as do these followers of "the god of this world." That is why suffering is an inevitability for us—and why godly people in both Testaments knew what it meant to suffer just as well as they knew what it meant to triumph. In his book, *Freedom of a Christian,* published back in 1520, Martin Luther made the statement, "The more Christian a man is, the more evils, sufferings, and deaths he must endure."[3] In *Christian Perfection* (published two centuries later in 1726), William Law said, "It would be strange to suppose that mankind were redeemed by the sufferings of the Saviour, to live in ease and softness themselves; that suffering should be necessary atonement for sin and yet that sinners should be excused from sufferings."

The marks of the Cross are not to be confused with self-inflicted austerity or the rigors of the Middle Ages brought up to date. We should not intentionally seek suffering or inflict it upon ourselves with the mistaken idea that we might thereby earn special merit with God. Asceticism is not necessarily a virtue. Christ admonished His followers: "When you fast, do not look somber as the hypocrites do, for they disfigure their faces to show men they are fasting" (Matt. 6:16). This was a clear warning not to boast of trials we have brought upon ourselves.

Bearing our cross does not mean wearing gunnysacks and a long face. What is required of us is not humiliation, but humility; not just thinking lowly of ourselves, but *not thinking of ourselves at all*.

Some people we meet imagine that every little headache is part of their cross. They become martyrs every time they hear criticism. Sometimes we deserve the criticism we receive. However, we are blessed only when men speak evil against us falsely *for Christ's sake*.

Lights for the Dark Days

Christians should be a foreign influence, a minority group in a pagan world. If the church is acceptable to this present age and is not stirring up trouble or suffering reproach, then it is not the true church that our Lord founded. We are the "light of the world"—and light exposes or shows things up. If we are at peace with this world, it may be because we have sold out to

---

3. Martin Luther, *Three Treatises, The Freedom of a Christian*, trans. W. A. Lambert, rev. Harold J. Grimm (Philadelphia: Fortress Press, 1960), p. 290.

it and compromised with it. Moody once said, "If the world has nothing to say against you, beware lest Jesus Christ has nothing to say for you."

The greatest testimony to this dark world today would be a band of crucified and risen men and women, dead to sin and alive unto God, bearing in their bodies "the marks of the Lord Jesus."

What the Bible Says about Suffering Believers

If you are a believer in Jesus Christ you are a "saint." The word is misunderstood today. This is a term which has been altered in modern vernacular to mean someone who is a sort of "super-Christian"; but in reality all of God's people are saints—"set apart" and dedicated to His service.

Anyone who reads the Bible and comes away thinking that suffering is not to be the lot of the Christian is reading the Scriptures blindly and without understanding. Here are some of the verses which speak clearly about the suffering in store for believers and the positive offer of divine help during times of suffering.

The psalmist said, "Many *are* the afflictions of the righteous: but the Lord delivereth him out of them all" (34:19, KJV). Note that the promise is "out of" not "from." The Living Bible puts it, "The good man does not escape all troubles—he has them too. But the Lord helps him in each and every one."

Speaking to His disciples at the end of His ministry and on the very eve of His death, Jesus said, "I have told you these things, so that in me you may have peace. In this world you will have trouble. But take heart! I have overcome the world" (John 16:33). Translate the word *trouble* as you will—difficulties, problems, pressures—Jesus unequivocally says the Christian will have it. But He also promises His presence with us *in* that trouble. In this case the implicit promise again is not *deliverance from* so much as it is *power to* overcome in the midst of whatever circumstances come our way. And *ultimately,* we know, our freedom from the wiles of the world will be total, for someday our Savior will again take over control of the world He created. For the present, Satan is its prince, but the Prince of Peace is scheduled to return—and His victory over Satan and his forces will be complete!

Expect Persecution

At the beginning of His Sermon on the Mount, Jesus included these words: "Blessed are those who are persecuted because of righteousness, for theirs is the kingdom of heaven. Blessed are you when people insult you, persecute you and falsely say all kinds of evil against you because of me. Rejoice and be glad, because great is your reward in heaven, for in the same way they persecuted the prophets who were before you" (Matt. 5:10–12). According to what Jesus is saying here, not only are we to *expect* persecution to be our lot as we follow the Christian way: we are to *rejoice* in those persecutions! Paul echoed that divine instruction when he wrote to the Philippians who were suffering for their faith, "Rejoice in the Lord always. I will say it again: Rejoice!" (4:4). They were to rejoice not only when the going was good, but *always!* Circumstances are not to color our reactions to persecution. Whenever as Christians we encounter trial and testing, we are to rejoice again and again, right to the end of our lives.

The apostle John in recording Christ's message to the church in Smyrna wrote, "Do not be afraid of what you are about to suffer. I tell you, the devil will put some of you in prison to test you, and you will suffer persecution . . . Be faithful, even to the point of death, and I will give you the crown of life" (Rev. 2:10).

Mysterious as it appears to be, true faith and suffering go hand in hand. You can't have the one without the other.

Again, it is difficult to understand that suffering is with God's permission, and many times we bring it upon ourselves. It is wrong to believe, for instance, that if you are sick it is because Satan has inflicted it upon you and if you have enough faith, it will go away. Sometimes God delivers, but not always; and when He permits suffering His grace is sufficient for you to endure it. He gives added strength. He walks hand in hand with you through your suffering, but He does not necessarily deliver you out of it.

Writing to Timothy, his young son in the faith, Paul said, "Everyone who wants to live a godly life in Christ Jesus *will be persecuted*" (2 Tim. 3:12, italics mine). That is putting it pretty bluntly! I think the principle is stated clearly so that you and I, as Christians, will not be in doubt. To be sure, some seem to suffer for their faith far more than others. Some of us have never known what it means to be physically persecuted for our faith, but all true Christians are subject to subtle suffering and insidious persecution. It may lie in the ridicule of our faith by those in the world around us. It could also exist in the discreet discrimination often practiced against Christian principles in the sophisticated arena of economics and society. For example, there are often discriminatory practices against the businessman, labor leader, or political figure trying to practice biblical, ethical, and moral standards.

Subtle persecution may happen to you in your office, school, or social gathering. You may not be "with it," or be "one of the crowd."

Points from Peter

In his first Epistle, the apostle Peter told his readers: "Dear friends, do not be surprised at the painful trial you are suffering, as though something strange were happening to you. But rejoice that you participate in the sufferings of Christ, so that you may be overjoyed when his glory is revealed. If you are insulted because of the name of Christ, you are blessed, for the Spirit of glory and of God rests on you. If you suffer, it should not be as a murderer or thief or any other kind of criminal, or even as a meddler. However, if you suffer as a Christian, do not be ashamed, but praise God that you bear that name. . . . So then, those who suffer according to God's will should commit themselves to their faithful Creator and continue to do good" (1 Pet. 4:12–19).

No suffering that the Christian endures for Christ is ever in vain. Living for Christ, walking in His way, is not an easy path—but it is a path to peace and power. The way of the Cross is a hard one, but it offers eternal rewards.

The scriptural principles relating to the endurance of pain

and persecution are just the same today as when they were
first set forth for us in the Word of God. Some of us may have
to die, or at least suffer, for our faith. The twentieth century
has seen more people tortured and killed for Christ than any
other century. Our generation has known its martyrs like Paul
Carlson, the missionary to the Congo who was killed trying to
rescue others. Jim Elliot was the young man who was killed,
along with four friends, trying to get the gospel to the Auca
Indians in Ecuador. Bishop Luwum was the Archbishop of the
Anglican Church of Uganda. He was shot in the head at point-
blank range.

Victorious Suffering

At the heart of our universe is a God who suffers in
redemptive love. We experience more of His love when we
suffer within an evil world. Someone has said that if one
suffers without succeeding, he can be sure that the success will
come in someone else's life. If he succeeds without suffering,
he can be equally sure that someone else has already suffered
for him.

High up in the foothills of the Himalayas is a beautiful city
called Kohima. It is in Nagaland, one of the states of India.
We were there to help them celebrate a hundred years of
Christianity. It was there that the Japanese were stopped in
their thrust toward India during World War II. Buried in a
cemetery are the bodies of hundreds of Indians, British,
Americans, and those of other nationalities who made up the
allied force that halted the Japanese advance. At the entrance
to the cemetery there is an engraved memorial which says,
"They gave their tomorrow that you might have today."

After sixteen difficult years as a missionary on the continent
of Africa, David Livingstone returned to his native Scotland to
address the students at Glasgow University. His body was
emaciated by the ravages of some twenty-seven fevers which
had coursed through his veins during the years of his service.
One arm hung useless at his side, the result of being mangled
by a lion. The core of his message to those young people was:
"Shall I tell you what sustained me amidst the toil, the

hardship, and loneliness of my exile? It was Christ's promise, 'Lo, I am with you always, even unto the end.'"

We, like David Livingstone, may claim the same promise from our Savior and Lord. He *does* go with us through our sufferings, and He awaits us as we emerge on the other side of the tunnel of testing—into the light of His glorious presence to live with Him forever!

*Storms make a strong tree, testings
make a strong Christian.*
ANONYMOUS

8/

Subtle Suffering

YOU MAY NEVER be called upon to suffer physically
because you are a believer in Jesus Christ. However, there is
more to suffering than physical pain; there is more to
persecution than being put in chains.

If we are followers of Jesus Christ, who are not compromis-
ing with the sinful ways of the world, we may be called upon to
suffer in subtle ways which are inescapable.

Suffering, in its many-shaped definitions, is a part of life in a
sinful world. Two Christians, recently released from a country
where the government was hostile toward Christianity, were
asked how it felt to be persecuted for their faith. They replied,
"We thought it was the normal way for a Christian to be
treated."

The Christian who expects to escape life's difficulties has an
unrealistic attitude and has failed to understand the Bible or
the history of the church.

We must suffer before we are rewarded. The concert pianist
or master musician knows he cannot escape the hours, days,
and months of grueling practice and self-sacrifice required
before the one hour of perfect performance.

The student cannot escape the years of struggle and study

before that great graduation day. The astronaut who hopes to participate in the space program knows it will require stern discipline to prepare for the exciting day on the launching pad.

The athlete who wants to be a member of the Olympic Team must count on years of training, discipline, and hard work. Several years ago a courageous and determined Japanese gymnast helped his team win a gold medal by performing some near-perfect gymnastic feats with a broken leg! Any star athlete will tell you that it takes pain and suffering to achieve success. But, as in the case of the Japanese gymnast, the pain and suffering are worth it!

If You Suffer

The apostle Peter has a tremendous passage on the subject of suffering:

> Dear friends, do not be surprised at the painful trial you are suffering, as though something strange were happening to you. . . . If you are insulted because of the name of Christ, you are blessed, for the Spirit of glory and of God rests on you. If you suffer, it should not be as a murderer or thief or any other kind of criminal, or even as a meddler. However, if you suffer as a Christian, do not be ashamed, but praise God that you bear that name. . . . So then, those who suffer according to God's will should commit themselves to their faithful Creator and continue to do good (1 Pet. 4:12,14,15,16,19).

Persecution has been a part of the heritage of the Jews throughout their long history, but in the passage quoted above Peter was writing to both Jews and Gentiles to help them understand what it means to suffer as a Christian.

It is never easy to be a Christian. The Christian life can still bring its own loneliness, unpopularity, and problems. It is human nature to dislike, resent, or regard with suspicion anyone who is "different." This is one of the great problems of the world today. Tribal differences, class differences, ethnic differences, cultural differences—these separate people. Such differences often lead not only to misunderstanding, but to war.

When the Christian brings the standards of Jesus Christ to

bear upon life in a materialistic and secularistic world, it is often resented. Because the moral and spiritual demands of Jesus Christ are so high, they often set the Christian "apart." This can bring about misunderstanding, fear, and resentment on the part of those in the Christian's cultural and ethnic group. When people do cross-cultural evangelism, they should learn to use methods in presenting the gospel and obeying the gospel that fit into the context of the lives of people of that culture. However, the redemptive, ethical, and moral aspects of the gospel can never be contextualized. They are the same in every culture, in every ethnic and racial grouping.

Persecution is also a test. One of the answers to the "why" of suffering is given in the Bible: "for a little while you may have had to suffer grief in all kinds of trials. These have come so that your faith—of greater worth than gold, which perishes even though refined by fire—may be proved genuine and may result in praise, glory and honor when Jesus Christ is revealed" (1 Pet. 1:6,7).

On June 16, A.D. 64, the great fire of Rome began. The Christians were blamed and persecuted. But Peter was not necessarily writing about those particular Christians. The ones he was writing to were suffering from reproach, lying, and slander. Peter was also looking ahead and saw the intense fiery trial shortly to come upon the church. I am convinced that the current popularity of evangelical Christianity in America will be short-lived. The Bible teaches, and history confirms it, that it never hurts the church to go through the furnace. Peter indicated that persecution is not a "strange" happening as far as Christians are concerned. He tells his readers, "Don't be surprised when it comes. Be surprised if it doesn't come!"

Abraham obeyed God and reached the Promised Land to find a famine. Jacob obeyed God and found his family turned against him. David obeyed God and hid in caves because King Saul sought his life. Paul obeyed God and found himself in prison. Paul said, "In fact, everyone who wants to live a godly life in Christ Jesus will be persecuted" (2 Tim. 3:12). Persecution for the Christian has many benefits, as we shall see later in this book. It gets us praying. It drives us deeper into the Scriptures. And it burns away the sins and the dross in our lives. Everybody of significance in the Bible went through it.

When you are identified with the name of Christ you will go through it. The Scriptures teach over and over that we need to be tested and purified.

We can take persecution because we know the purpose behind it. The purpose is to glorify God. Sixteen times in 1 Peter the apostle talks about the glory of God. He says in effect: I'll tell you what you really need. Go through the furnace, and when you go through the furnace to the glory of God, the Spirit of God comes upon you, and there is a joy in your heart and you glorify God.

Through persecution we also partake of the sufferings of Jesus Christ. When a man has to suffer and sacrifice for his faith, he is walking the way Christ walked, and sharing the cross that Christ carried. The Scriptures teach that if we "share in his sufferings . . . we may also share in his glory" (Rom. 8:17). In Philippians 3:10 Paul says, "I want to know Christ and the power of his resurrection and the fellowship of sharing in his sufferings, becoming like him in his death." Many times Paul returns to the thought that when the Christian has to suffer he is in some strange way sharing in the very sufferings of Christ and is even filling up the sufferings of Christ (2 Cor. 1:5; 4:10,11; Gal. 6:17; Col. 1:24).

To suffer for the faith is not a penalty; it is a privilege. In doing so, we share in the very work and ministry of Christ. If we are united with Christ and His sufferings, we will also be united with Christ in His resurrection. To know Christ is to become so identified with Him that we share His every experience. It "means that we share the way he walked; we share the Cross he bore; we share the death he died; and finally we share the life he lives forevermore."[1]

However, it is also wonderful to think that in our Christian life the power of His resurrection precedes the fellowship of His sufferings. In other words, the power of His resurrection is available to us from day to day through the Holy Spirit. We enjoy the sense of God's presence in the midst of suffering here and now. I have talked to people who are experiencing deep pain or severe difficulties, and they have said, "I feel

---

1. William Barclay, *The Letters to the Philippians, Colossians, and Thessalonians* (Philadelphia: Westminster Press, 1975), p. 64.

God is so close to me." When Stephen was on trial for his life and when it was certain that he would be condemned to death, his face appeared to the onlookers as if it were the face of an angel (Acts 6:15).

When the three Hebrew children were thrown into the fiery furnace and the king looked in, he saw a fourth who was like unto the "Son of God" (Dan. 3:25, KJV). No believer is ever left to suffer alone. Christ is always present with him.

There is a legend of a pioneer missionary to some distant island who led his first convert to Christ. Later this man was tortured to death by his fellow natives. Years later when the missionary himself had died and gone to glory, he met this martyred convert and asked him how it felt to be tortured to death for Christ. The man looked at him a moment and then replied, "You know, I don't remember!"

To suffer as a Christian takes many different forms. Some persecutions may be of the more subtle types.

In His Sermon on the Mount, Jesus said, "Blessed are those who are persecuted because of righteousness, for theirs is the kingdom of heaven" (Matt. 5:10). What did He mean? Jesus could have been including the "hassle" Christians encounter in the world, simply because there are those worldlings who see a different life style which distinguishes believers as aliens in modern society. This makes the non-Christian feel guilty or antagonistic.

How different are you? Is there anything that distinguishes you from the secularist, the agnostic, or the atheist? In His parable of the sower, Jesus describes those who fail to maintain their stand for the right: "Since he has no root, he lasts only a short time. When trouble or *persecution* comes because of the word, he quickly falls away" (Matt. 13:21, italics mine).

However, Jesus makes it clear that there is a reward for faithfulness in the face of persecution or deprivation. "'I tell you the truth,'" Jesus told Peter, "'no one who has left home or brothers or sisters or mother or father or children or fields for me and the gospel will fail to receive a hundred times as much in this present age (homes, brothers, sisters, mothers, children and fields—and with them, persecutions) and in the age to come, eternal life'" (Mark 10:29,30).

In very plain terms Jesus reminds His disciples in John 15:20: "Remember the words I spoke to you: 'No servant is greater than his master.' If they persecuted me, they will persecute you also." When we are persecuted for our faith, we are in good company!

Persecution by Insults

Jesus also warned His followers, "Blessed are you when people insult you, persecute you and falsely say all kinds of evil against you because of me" (Matt. 5:11). Likewise the apostle Peter wrote: "If you are insulted because of the name of Christ, you are blessed, for the Spirit of glory and of God rests on you" (1 Pet. 4:14). Insults often come as a result of a Christian's life style, which is different from that of the secular world.

What do you mean by life style? This subject is being given a good deal of attention by the church throughout the world. An older British Christian at Oxford told me that when he was a boy, it was looked upon as a sin for a Christian to gamble, drink, dance, go to the movies, or for a girl to wear makeup. He said that was the "legalism" of that generation. He went on to say that the new legalism of this era involves "life style." The new vogue says that if you drive a decent car, wear good clothes, or enjoy some of the creature comforts of life, your Christian walk may be "judged" by other Christians. I believe this is just as legalistic as saying that a Christian girl should not wear makeup.

I believe that life style, in the biblical sense, means that the Christian does not practice things like lying, dishonesty, greed, jealousy, pride, prejudice. He does not condone social injustice. He is dominated by love, joy, and peace in his inward life. He has a genuine love for his neighbor. He takes unpopular stands on moral and social issues. He has a God-given grace to forgive those who do him wrong. He may be firm in his theological, moral and ethical concepts, but he is tolerant of those who sincerely hold other views. I believe that *that* is the basic life style the Scriptures are talking about.

Outward life styles are "relative" from country to country

and from culture to culture. We must allow other Christians freedom of conscience in moral issues about which the Bible is not clear.

A great Christian friend of mine who belongs to the so-called "Plymouth Brethren" in Europe was entertaining some American Christian friends who he knew did not drink alcohol. He was serving wine and soft drinks. He laughingly said, "I serve wine to the glory of Christ, and you refuse it to the glory of Christ—and we are both right." There are different customs and traditions in different parts of the world and we should not be judgmental on such things.

I remember when we first went to Ireland in 1946 some Irish Christians were appalled when they heard that my wife used a little makeup. For Christians to use makeup was against the legalism of that day among certain groups of Christians.

If insults come as a result of inward convictions and attitude, then we have a cause to rejoice. If, however, we criticize or insult each other over cultural differences on which the Bible is not explicit, then we are not recognizing one another's freedom to choose.

Persecuted with Gossip and Slander

From the subtleties of insults to the active arena of gossip and slander is just one small step. I am talking here about the attitudes directed against Christians by non-Christians. Discrimination may be strong against the Christian who is "living out" his beliefs. "If you suffer, it should not be as a murderer or thief or any other kind of criminal, or even as a meddler. However, if you suffer as a Christian, do not be ashamed, but praise God that you bear that name" (1 Pet. 4:15,16).

Jesus said, "It is enough for the student to be like his teacher, and the servant like his master. If the head of the house has been called Beelzebub, how much more the members of his household!" (Matt. 10:25). Jesus suffered persecution and harassment; how can we, His followers, expect to escape?

Paul knew what it meant to encounter the jealousy and hatred of the people in Pisidian Antioch. As the crowd gathered to hear him preach, the religious leaders were "filled with jealousy and talked abusively against what Paul was saying" (Acts 13:45).

Peter prophesied the same kind of treatment for the Christian: "They think it strange that you do not plunge with them into the same flood of dissipation, and they heap abuse on you" (1 Pet. 4:4).

Is there a Christian student at college or university who hasn't been verbally abused because he wouldn't join his peers in a drinking or sex party? Is there a Christian businessman who has never lost an account because he wouldn't take the kickback under the table? Is there a Christian laborer who has conscientiously earned his wages who hasn't been ridiculed by some of his peers for not cheating on the job? Is there a Christian traveling salesman who is honest in his expense accounts who hasn't been laughed at or scorned in some way by his fellow salesmen because of his honesty? It costs in a thousand subtle ways to be a true disciple of Christ.

False Accusations

Jesus told His disciples, "Blessed are you when people . . . falsely say all kinds of evil against you because of me" (Matt. 5:11). Note the word "falsely." It is nothing to our credit if people can truthfully accuse us of inconsistent conduct as Christian believers. Our life must correspond with our profession. What Jesus is talking about is *false* accusations.

Jesus Himself was subject to false accusations at His trial. He was charged with blasphemy when He stood before the Jewish Council and with sedition when he faced Pontius Pilate. Both charges were false.

The apostles Peter and John were falsely accused when they in turn were brought before the Council (or Sanhedrin). They were charged with wrongdoing when in fact their only "crime" was that in the name of the Lord Jesus they had healed a lame man (Acts 4:8–12).

Stephen, the first Christian martyr, faced false accusations when he, too, was arraigned before the Council (Acts 7). Paul and Silas at Philippi were also wrongly accused, beaten, and flung into prison (Acts 16). The same sort of thing happened to Paul again and again in his later missionary travels.

If the apostles and other early church leaders were falsely accused because of their faith, how can we present-day Christians expect to escape false accusations and the hurt which such attacks can bring into our lives?

Rejection by Others

Probably one of the forms of persecution which hurts us most is that of *rejection*. Basically, we all want to be accepted and loved. Instead, we may find ourselves spurned and cast off. Jesus Himself is the supreme example of experiencing rejection. "He was despised and rejected by men" (Isa. 53:3). "He came to that which was his own, but his own did not receive him" (John 1:11).

In Matthew 10:14 He told His disciples, "If anyone will not welcome you or listen to your words, shake the dust off your feet when you leave that home or town." Many times Paul and his missionary companions met with opposition and persecution as they entered various cities on their evangelistic journeys. However, Paul followed his Master's advice in handling rejection, and we are to do the same. Shake the dust off your feet and move on. Rejection should not lead to discouragement but to action.

Samuel Rutherford, the saintly Scottish pastor and theologian, once said, "Through many afflictions we must enter into the kingdom of God. . . . It is folly to think to steal to heaven with a whole skin."

Hatred from Others and Even the Family

Not only must the Christian be prepared to face rejection and hatred in the world. The members of his own family circle may turn against him. In Matthew 10:21–23, Jesus told His disciples:

Brother will betray brother to death, and a father his child; children will rebel against their parents and have them put to death. All men will hate you because of me, but he who stands firm to the end will be saved. When you are persecuted in one place, flee to another.

This prediction has been proven many times throughout history. How descriptive it is of Christians who have lived under oppressive atheistic regimes, when parents would be betrayed by children or brothers would report brothers.

Samuel Rutherford was referring to this kind of suffering when he wrote: "I think not much of a cross when all the children of the house weep with me and for me; and to suffer when we enjoy the communion of saints is not much; but it is hard when saints rejoice in the suffering of saints, and redeemed ones hurt (yea, even go nigh to hate) redeemed ones."

Unconverted members of the family, as well as society at large, sometimes hate anyone who has embraced the gospel. In my travels I have met many people who have suffered under the bitter hostility of blood relatives.

I was on an airliner in the Far East when one of the stewards asked if he could talk to me. He had a big smile on his face when he said, "I have been a Christian for two years. I came from a non-Christian background. My family belonged to a religious sect which was quite opposed to Christianity. Yet for years I had been searching for something. I didn't know what it was. One day I listened to a tape of a preacher who told about Jesus Christ. I knew this was what I had been searching for all of my life. I accepted Christ, went home and told my parents, brothers, and sisters about my new-found faith. They beat me and threw me out of the house. However, I continued to witness to them and now, I am glad to say, they are all Christians."

In John 15:18–21, Jesus describes why the world, and even the Christian's unbelieving family, takes this attitude toward the faithful follower of Christ. Someone may ask what I mean by the "world." The word bears a number of different meanings in the Bible. In the present context it means the world system, the political and social order organized apart from God, so often dominated by evil.

Jesus told His disciples:

If the world hates you, keep in mind that it hated me first. If you belonged to the world, it would love you as its own. As it is, you do not belong to the world, but I have chosen you out of the world. That is why the world hates you. Remember the words I spoke to you: "No servant is greater than his master." If they persecuted me, they will persecute you also. If they obeyed my teaching, they will obey yours also. They will treat you this way because of my name, for they do not know the One who sent me.

However, there is no need to be depressed over the trials we have to suffer or through fear of persecution. As Christians, I think we sometimes tend to forget that we have a companion in our struggles. It reminds me of a story printed by Ann Landers in her column and repeated across the country in various media:

One night I dreamed I was walking along the beach with the Lord. Many scenes from my life flashed across the sky. In each scene I noticed footprints in the sand. Sometimes there were two sets of footprints, other times there was only one.

This bothered me because I noted that during the low periods of my life, when I was suffering from anguish, sorrow or defeat, I could see only one set of footprints, so I said to the Lord, "You promised me, Lord, that if I followed you, you would walk with me always. But I have noticed that during the most trying periods of my life there has been only one set of footprints in the sand. Why, when I have needed you most, have you not been there for me?"

The Lord replied, "The times when you have seen only one set of footprints, my child, is when I carried you."

Paul's Irritations

The apostle Paul was called upon to suffer for Christ, but through it all he had in the Holy Spirit a supernatural resource which kept him victorious. Not only was he called upon to suffer physically, but he also met the more subtle suffering of being made to appear foolish in the eyes of other men. He describes his experiences in 1 Corinthians 4:9–13:

For it seems to me that God has put us apostles on display at the end of the procession, like men condemned to die in the arena. We have been made a spectacle to the whole universe, to angels as well as to men. We are fools for Christ, but you are so wise in Christ! We are weak, but you are strong! You are honored, we are dishonored! To this very hour we go hungry and thirsty, we are in rags, we are brutally treated, we are homeless. We work hard with our own hands. When we are cursed, we bless; when we are persecuted, we endure it; when we are slandered, we answer kindly. Up to this moment we have become the scum of the earth, the refuse of the world.

Paul tells us in 2 Corinthians of the troubles, hardships, beatings, sleeplessness, and other sufferings which the servants of God were called upon to endure. As he thought about his responsibilities as a Christian missionary, he also said, "I face daily the pressure of my concern for all the churches" (2 Cor. 11:28).

How vividly Paul's concern for the churches brings out the great pressure upon Christian leadership. The responsibilities of the ministry can often be overwhelming. Humanly speaking, it can lead to loneliness, depression, and often discouragement. But, in the midst of it all, is God's illimitable grace and His peace which passes all understanding.

Being a well-known clergyman in these days of "media" exposure brings pressures that the average Christian could not begin to understand. In my own case the pressures at times, mentally, physically, and spiritually, have become so great that I have almost wished the Lord would take me home now. I want to escape or flee. But I know that God has called me to my responsibilities, and I must be faithful. As an example of what I mean, there is the problem of being quoted continually in the press, with the consequent danger that one might say the wrong thing or that what was said might be misinterpreted and bring reproach to the name of Christ. People put well-known Christians on a pedestal, and if the slightest thing goes wrong, they are immediately blamed and often ridiculed by their fellow Christians. This is part of what Paul meant when he talked about "the care of all the churches" resting upon him. This was an even greater pressure on Paul than the physical sufferings he endured. I have often wondered what would have happened in the ministry of the Lord Jesus Christ if television had been in existence. What would they have done, for example, with the raising of Lazarus or the healing of Bartimaeus or the feeding of the 5,000?

We may never be called upon to suffer as Paul did. Nevertheless, how triumphant we can be with an attitude like his: "We are hard pressed on every side, but not crushed; perplexed, but not in despair; persecuted, but not abandoned; struck down, but not destroyed" (2 Cor. 4:8,9).

God has never sent any difficulty into the life of His children without His accompanying offers of help in this life and reward in the life to come.

Whatever affliction comes in our life, our Lord goes into the valley with us, leading us by the hand, even carrying us when it is necessary.

Here is a verse to memorize and repeat:

No temptation has seized you except what is common to man. And God is faithful; he will not let you be tempted beyond what you can bear. But when you are tempted, he will also provide a way out [of escape] so that you can stand up under it (1 Cor. 10:13).

I do not pray for a lighter load but for a stronger back.

PHILLIPS BROOKS

9/

Living above Your Circumstances

TO THOSE OF US who are sighted, blindness could be an overwhelming handicap. For most of her ninety-five years on earth, Fanny Crosby was blind. Yet she had the deep spiritual perception to write such classic Christian hymns as "Saved by Grace" and hundreds of other hymns and gospel songs that have inspired and comforted Christians for a hundred years.

In more recent times, Ken Medema, the blind singer and songwriter whose whimsical tunes and happy lyrics have made him beloved across America, has turned his handicap into a joyous celebration of the goodness of God.

John Milton wrote the immortal *Paradise Lost* as a result of the shattering experience of blindness. This classic glorifies and extolls the greatness of God.

The renowned missionary to the American Indians, David Brainerd, and the famous Scottish clergyman, Robert Murray McCheyne, were both afflicted with lung diseases and died before the age of thirty. And yet, young as they were, both established themselves in the forefront of Christian service and were noted for their holy living.

Louis Pasteur, the French chemist who discovered the germ-killing process which has been called "pasteurizing," was semi-paralyzed and subject to epileptic seizures. He never gave up on his search for solutions to the diseases so rampant in his lifetime. It is possible that if he had known good health he might have forsaken his research for more lucrative work.

Beethoven was compelled by increasing deafness to abandon his intended career as a pianist and to concentrate on the writing of music. As a result, he became one of the greatest composers of all time.

I am convinced that there is a blessing in suffering. It is not always possible to see the blessing in the particular problem we face, but suffering can and does serve a positive purpose. In spite of their handicaps and pain, the people we have just cited achieved great things to the benefit of mankind because they learned to live above their circumstances. With God's help we can do the same.

Problems in life come to everyone whether to a greater or lesser degree. As the "Music Man" said, "There's trouble in River City." Trials make some people bitter, and other people better. Why the difference?

The psalmist provides the answer in Psalm 43:5. The difference is faith in God. "Why are you downcast, O my soul? Why so disturbed within me? Put your hope in God."

The Hope Road

The apostle Paul was a great exponent of hope. "Christ in you, the hope of glory" (Col. 1:27). In writing those words he pins our hope on Christ; and what better hope is there than Christ "in you"? If He is in your heart, He brings with Him all the blessings of His Spirit: love, joy, peace, and the other positive fruit that is to be apparent in the believer's life (Gal. 5:22,23). Hearing the message of the verses from the Scriptures, the Christian may have a glimpse of what his life *can* be if it is truly yielded to Christ's control.

Think of some of the implications of having Christ in you—
1. you will never be alone again;
2. you can "cast all your anxiety on him because he cares for you" (1 Pet. 5:7);
3. you can count on the fruit of the Spirit growing in your life;
4. you can count on having one or more gifts of the Spirit to use for the advancement of God's kingdom.

Thus you will not only have "hope in heaven," but you will also have "hope" for each day of this earthly life despite outward circumstances and the difficulties that may be created by your situation.

This is just a part of the spiritual legacy that is ours as we "hope in God" and experience the reality of "Christ in you, the hope of glory." The broad vistas of victorious living into which this door of "hope" leads us are too vast to contemplate, too deep to comprehend. But they await the believer who obeys the command to "hope"!

Paul's Thorn in the Flesh

The apostle Paul, by firsthand experience, knew what it meant to suffer. As he was telling the people of Corinth about some of his exalted personal experiences with the risen Lord, he confessed that he had a real physical problem: "To keep me from becoming conceited because of these surpassingly great revelations, there was given me a thorn in my flesh, a messenger of Satan, to torment me" (2 Cor. 12:7).

We don't know exactly what that "thorn in the flesh" was, but it must have been a physical ailment. It may have been some type of eye disease or epilepsy; or, as Sir William Ramsay thought most likely, malarial fever. Some have suggested it might have been chronic insomnia—though I think it unlikely. However, we do know how he handled his problem and what his subsequent attitude toward it was:

> Three times I pleaded with the Lord to take it away from me. But he said to me, "My grace is sufficient for you, for my power is made perfect in weakness." Therefore I will boast all the more gladly about my weaknesses, so that Christ's power may rest on me. That is why, for Christ's sake, I delight in weaknesses, in insults, in hardships, in persecutions, in difficulties. For when I am weak, then I am strong (2 Cor. 12:8–10).

Certainly Paul did not like that thorn in the flesh. But when he knew that it was not possible to get rid of it, he stopped groaning and began glorifying. He knew it was God's will and that the affliction was an opportunity for him to prove the power of Christ in his life.

Paul also knew what it was to suffer from circumstances outside himself. He literally boasts about the suffering he endured at the hands of those who persecuted him. He was whipped, beaten with rods, stoned, and shipwrecked; he suffered cold and hunger; he was betrayed by friends. Any one of those circumstances would have defeated most of us. However, Paul concludes his catalog of sufferings with these triumphant words which we should imprint upon our hearts: "When I am weak, then I am strong."

Would you be able to live above your circumstances as Paul did? To withstand suffering as severe as his in our own power would be impossible. Yet with the apostle we can say, "I can do everything through him who gives me strength" (Phil. 4:13).

Stephen, the First Martyr

How could a blessing come out of a murder? Stephen was another New Testament character who suffered and died for the cause of Christ, and his martyrdom resulted in the advancement of the gospel.

Stephen was chosen from the early disciples in Jerusalem to fulfill the task of a deacon. Under his ministry, as well as that of the apostles themselves, "the word of God spread. The number of disciples in Jerusalem increased rapidly, and a large number of priests became obedient to the faith" (Acts 6:7).

Stephen was "a man full of God's grace and power" whose witness soon began to tell. As a result he began to face opposition. Any person who speaks out boldly for the Lord Jesus Christ will encounter strong resistance. "Opposition arose, . . . men began to argue with Stephen, but they could not stand up against his wisdom or the Spirit by which he spoke" (Acts 6:9,10).

The upshot of it all was that the religious leaders aroused the people to bring Stephen to trial before the Council. False charges were laid against him by lying witnesses, and he was sentenced to death by stoning.

As he was dying, Stephen looked up and declared that he saw Jesus standing at the right hand of God. This infuriated the mob into such a frenzy that they bore down on Stephen with added vengeance.

"While they were stoning him, Stephen prayed, 'Lord Jesus, receive my spirit.' Then he fell on his knees and cried out,

'Lord, do not hold this sin against them.' When he had said this, he fell asleep" (Acts 7:59,60).

There is an interesting footnote to this story. A man named Saul watched as this bloody murder took place. He, of course, was later to become the apostle Paul. I believe that Stephen's conduct at his trial, his stirring sermon, and his courageous martyrdom may have been among the factors which later influenced Saul to come to Christ himself.

Job: Not a Fair-weather Saint

Out of the many suffering saints in the Old Testament, two stand out for me; one of them is almost a classic illustration of suffering. We often speak of "the patience of Job," and by that we mean his patient endurance of the excruciating suffering he was called upon to experience. His triumphant attitude is even more amazing when we realize what happened to him. His suffering was more than just physical—

1. he lost his health;
2. he lost his wealth;
3. he lost his children.

Job was reduced to sitting amidst the rubble of his once-prosperous life. And after the loss of everything he held worthwhile, still he could say, "Though he [God] slay me, yet will I hope in him" (Job 13:15). Later, he voiced that ringing declaration, "I know that my Redeemer lives, and that in the end he will stand upon the earth" (19:25). These words came from the lips of a man who was crushed in mind and body from the suffering he had endured at the hands of Satan.

After the worst of his troubles, his wife said to him, "Are you still holding on to your integrity? Curse God and die!" In spite of those strong words, Job replied: "You are talking like a foolish [denoting moral deficiency] woman. Shall we accept good from God, and not trouble?" We go on to read that "in all this, Job did not sin in what he said" (Job 2:9,10).

Job was not perfect. Note the Bible says he "did not sin in what he *said*"! However, he is a towering model for us to follow in our attitude toward suffering. Despite his difficulties, he could say, "The Lord gave and the Lord has taken away; may the name of the Lord be praised" (Job 1:21).

The Book of Job does not solve the problem of suffering, but it teaches some valuable lessons. For one thing, it makes clear that the innocent suffer as well as the guilty and that virtue is not always rewarded here on earth. Job's sufferings were unmerited. He rejected the accusations of his three friends and maintained his integrity. Nor did God accuse him of having done wrong.

Again, the story helps us to distinguish between *retributive* and *disciplinary* suffering. God was not punishing Job, but testing his faith and refining his character. Job emerged from his ordeal a better and wiser man.

Job's story has a glorious conclusion. You can find it in the forty-second chapter of Job, but here are the highlights:

> After Job had prayed for his friends [those who had maligned him throughout his testing experience], the Lord made him prosperous again and gave him twice as much as he had before. All his brothers and sisters . . . comforted and consoled him over all the trouble the Lord had brought upon him, . . . The Lord blessed the latter part of Job's life more than the first (vv.10–12).

What a testimony Job is to the ultimate faithfulness of God to His own children!

In his book, *Where Is God When It Hurts?*, Philip Yancey says: "Satan had taunted God with the accusation that humans are not truly free, because God had weighted Job's rewards so he would choose in His favor. Was Job being faithful because God had allowed him such a prosperous life? The test proved he was not. Job is an eternal example of one who stayed faithful to God even though his world caved in and it seemed as though God Himself had turned against him. Job clung to God's justice when, apparently, he was the best example in history of God's alleged injustice. He did not seek the Giver because of His gifts; when all gifts were removed he still sought the Giver."[1]

---

1. Philip Yancey, *Where Is God When It Hurts?* (Grand Rapids: Zondervan, 1977), p. 69.

From Prison to Palace

There is another Old Testament character who provides us with an illustration of suffering, namely, Joseph. His brothers plotted to kill him, and sold him into slavery. He was separated at a young age from his family and sent to a strange land. As a young man he was accused falsely of trying to seduce his master's wife, and, as a consequence, was cast into prison. These events were enough to throw any man into despair.

Someone has said: "God never uses anybody to a large degree, until after he breaks that one all to pieces." Joseph had more sorrow than all the other sons of Jacob, yet he was faithful. His faithfulness in suffering led him to be Prime Minister of Egypt. As a result of his position and power, he was able to save his family from famine. For this reason the Holy Spirit said of him, "Joseph is a fruitful vine, a fruitful vine near a spring, whose branches climb over a wall" (Gen. 49:22).

It takes suffering to widen the soul.

Suffering in Our Modern World

The list is endless of those who have suffered for Christ since the days of the early church. We read about Catholics and Protestants alike who in centuries past suffered terrible things for their loyalty to their faith. Most of these valiant Christians died under torture and were subjected to inhuman treatment that staggers the imagination.

But we don't have to go back so far in history. The twentieth century has witnessed some of the most appalling examples of mass suffering in the history of the human race. Millions have suffered and died in two catastrophic world wars, with millions more perishing in numerous other wars and revolutions. Several years ago I visited the infamous Nazi death camp of Auschwitz, where several million people (both Jews and non-Jews) were mercilessly slaughtered. I cannot begin to describe the feelings of horror and revulsion which swept over me as I walked through that stark monument to man's inhumanity to man.

Or again, our century has repeatedly witnessed incredible scenes of mass hunger and starvation in many parts of the world. No sincere Christian can remain indifferent to such tragic events. The desperate plight of the poor and starving, the widespread toleration of economic and social injustices, the mindless escalation of weapons of mass destruction—these and countless other problems vividly demonstrate that we live in a world where evil and suffering are not only real, but are ever increasing. These problems also challenge all Christians to pray and work to alleviate suffering and to combat the causes of these problems wherever possible.

As Christians, we know that all suffering and evil will never be eliminated from our world until Christ comes again. But we also know Christ commands us to do all we can to demonstrate His love for all those who suffer. We are to fight evil and injustice and work in the name of Christ for the welfare of others.

But suffering affects all kinds and classes of individuals every day. Suffering in scores of forms can be found all around us. One has only to go to the slums of New York, the hospitals of any city, or the homes where family life has tragically broken up. Talk to the millions of children who are living with only one parent or no parent. Talk to the tens of thousands of patients who have been notified that they have cancer or heart disease. Talk to the victims of the muggings, rapes, and other crimes that go on daily in almost every city. Go to the prisons and talk to the prisoners who are paying the bitter price of their wrong-doing. Talk to pastors whose hearts are breaking because members of their congregations profess one thing and live another. The whole world is crying for help.

One person whose name is synonymous with "victorious suffering" is the courageous, gifted quadraplegic girl, Joni Eareckson. She is confined to a wheelchair, unable to care for her simplest needs, and yet she is one of the most vibrant, beautiful human beings I have known.

She has shared the platform with us many times in our crusades, and her testimony to what the Lord has done for her in and through her testing never ceases to amaze and humble me. Joni has emerged from the fire of her testing with an unbelievably broad and perceptive insight into not only the meaning of suffering, but also into all the great theological truths that bear on this subject. Joni has had her own small armageddon.

Her ability to grasp the deepest truths and phrase them in simple terms awes and inspires me. I know of very few people, including some of our greatest theologians, who have such a practical and wide-ranging grasp of who God is and what He is doing in His world. Her books and the film on her life, her appearances on television, and her story in the press have touched the lives of millions. Her service for God is many times greater than if she had never had that accident while diving into the Chesapeake Bay.

Kim Wickes, who comes to most of our crusades, was a little girl, blinded because the retinas of her eyes had been destroyed when she looked at a bomb blast. Her father tried to kill her by throwing her into a river. Desperate and at his wit's end from war and starvation, Kim's father eventually left her at a home for deaf and blind children in Taegu, Korea. Later she was adopted by some Americans and began the years of study and training which have resulted in a testimony in word and song which has thrilled millions. Her studies have taken her to the finest schools in the world, including study in Vienna. The events in Kim's life could have destroyed many people, but by God's grace she has triumphed over adversity.

Today there are thousands of Christians all over the world who are facing daily pain, persecution, and opposition for their faith. We are now learning of their triumph and survival in many parts of the world. Their faith in Christ is deep and strong. Their willingness to face persecution puts us to shame.

I do not understand how the human body can withstand such persecution as some of our brothers and sisters in Christ are experiencing today—such as in Uganda. I only know that when Jesus Christ is with a person, that one can endure the deepest suffering and somehow emerge a better and stronger Christian because of it. The question of *how* we are to endure suffering is dealt with in the next chapter.

The Supreme Sufferer: Jesus Christ

Do we look at ourselves, our trials, our problems, when we are suffering? Do we live under the circumstances, instead of above the circumstances? Or do we look at the One who knew more suffering than we are able to conceive?

In *Table Talk* Martin Luther said, "Our suffering is not worthy the name of suffering. When I consider my crosses, tribulations, and temptations, I shame myself almost to death, thinking what are they in comparison of the sufferings of my blessed Saviour Jesus Christ."

There are several things about the life of Christ that reveal His role as the "suffering servant" Messiah. We cannot begin to trace every aspect of this search through His life, but consider these truths:

In Isaiah 53 the sufferings of the Savior are so minutely pictured that one might well read it as the record of an eyewitness, rather than the prediction of a man who wrote eight hundred years before the event.

Observe that *Jesus' life began in the midst of persecution and peril.* He came on a mission of love and mercy, sent by the Father. An angel announced His conception and gave Him His name. The heavenly host sang a glorious anthem at His birth. By the extraordinary "star" or meteor, the very heavens indicated His coming. In Himself He was the most illustrious child ever born—the holy child of Mary, the divine Son of God. Yet no sooner did He enter our world than Herod decreed His death and labored to accomplish it.

Notice, too, that *He assumed a role of deep abasement.* The Son of the eternal Father, He became the infant of days and was made in the likeness of man. He assumed our human nature with all its infirmities, and weakness, and capacity for suffering. He came as a child of the poorest parents. His entire life was one voluntary humiliation. He came to be a servant and to minister rather than to be ministered unto.

Another aspect of His suffering is the *vile suspicions and bitter misrepresentations* He had to bear. "He came to that which was his own, but his own did not receive him" (John 1:11). Rather they scorned Him and treated Him with contempt. He was "despised and rejected" by most of them. They treated Him as a transgressor of God's law, a Sabbath-breaker, an unholy person—a winebibber and drunkard, one who associated with outcasts and notorious sinners.

Notice also that *He was constantly exposed to personal violence.* At the beginning of His ministry, His own townsfolk at Nazareth tried to hurl Him down from the brow of the hill (Luke 4:29). The religious and political leaders often conspired to seize Him and kill Him. At length He was arrested and brought to trial before Pilate and Herod. Even though He was guiltless of the accusations, He was denounced as an enemy of God and man, and not worthy to live.

The sufferings of Jesus also included *the fierce temptations of the devil.* The account of this transaction is given in graphic form in Matthew 4:1, "Then Jesus was led by the Spirit into the desert to be tempted by the devil."

Remember, too, that *He knew in advance what was coming,* and this enhanced His suffering. He knew the contents of the cup He had to drink; He knew the path of suffering He should tread. He could distinctly foresee the baptism of blood that awaited Him. He spoke plainly to His disciples of His coming death by crucifixion.

Jesus, the supreme sufferer, *came to suffer for our sins.* As a result of His sufferings, our redemption was secured.

What does the divine sufferer demand from us? Only our faith, our love, our grateful praise, our consecrated hearts and lives. Is that too much to ask?

Christ living in us will enable us to live above our circumstances, however painful they are. Perhaps you who read these words find yourself almost crushed by the circumstances which you are now facing. You wonder how much more you can stand. But don't despair! God's grace is sufficient for you and will enable you to rise above your trials. Let this be your confidence:

> Who shall separate us from the love of Christ? Shall trouble or hardship or persecution or famine or nakedness or danger or sword? . . . No, in all these things we are more than conquerors through him who loved us (Rom. 8:35–37).

> *Pain, God's megaphone, can drive me away from Him. I can hate God for allowing such misery. Or, on the other hand, it can drive me to Him.*[1]
>
> PHILIP YANCEY

10/

What Do I Do with My Pain?

WE ARE NOT always consistent in our reactions to personal suffering. With one type of affliction we may manage to bear up and keep going. With another of life's blows we may seem to fall apart.

Our Reactions Are a Result of Our Convictions

Lord George Gordon Byron and Sir Walter Scott were gifted writers and poets who lived in the late eighteenth and early nineteenth centuries. They were both lame. Byron bitterly resented his infirmity and constantly grumbled about his lot in life. Scott was never heard to complain about his handicap.

One day Scott received a letter from Byron which said, "I would give my fame to have your happiness." What made the difference in their reactions to suffering and their attitudes toward their disabilities? Byron was a man who took pride in his dissolute life style. His moral standards were doubtful.

---

1. Philip Yancey, *Where Is God When It Hurts?* (Grand Rapids: Zondervan, 1977), p. 57.

Scott, on the other hand, was a Christian believer whose courageous life exemplified his Christian standards and values.

For the Christian, the reaction to suffering should be influenced by his concept of what Jesus Christ endured for him on the cross and his understanding of the will of God for him in his pain, no matter what its source or intensity.

The Christian life is a life free from the *penalty* of sin so far as judgment is concerned, but it is not free from the *results* of sin. Because of man's disobedience in the Garden, sin has invaded God's perfect universe, and hence the inevitable suffering we encounter during our human pilgrimage—suffering which will end, as far as the cosmos is concerned, at Armageddon. Meanwhile, we are not free from heartache, sickness, emotional upheaval, financial problems, and the whole spectrum of human suffering.

Christ Never Promised the Easy Life

Jesus Christ spoke frankly to His disciples about the future. He hid nothing from them. No one could ever accuse Him of deception or making false promises.

In unmistakable language, He told them that discipleship meant a life of self-denial and the bearing of a cross. He asked them to count the cost carefully, lest they should turn back when they met with suffering and privation.

Jesus told His followers that the world would hate them. They would be arrested, scourged, and brought before governors and kings. Even their loved ones would persecute them. As the world hated Him, so it would treat His servants. He also warned, "a time is coming when anyone who kills you will think he is offering a service to God" (John 16:2).

The Christian therefore must expect conflict, not an easy, cozy life. He is a soldier, and as it has been said, his captain never promised him immunity from the hazards of battle.

Many of Christ's early followers were disappointed in Him, for, in spite of His warnings, they expected Him to subdue their enemies and set up a world political kingdom. When they came face to face with reality, they "turned back and no longer followed him" (John 6:66). But the true disciples of Jesus all suffered for their faith.

We are told that the early Christians went rejoicing to their deaths, as if they were going to a marriage feast. They bathed their hands in the blaze kindled for them and shouted with gladness. One early historian, witnessing their heroism, wrote, "When the day of victory dawned, the Christians marched in procession from the prison to the arena as if they were marching to heaven, with joyous countenances agitated by gladness rather than fear."

Tacitus, a Roman historian, writing of the early Christian martyrs, said, "Mockery of every sort was added to their deaths. Covered with the skins of beasts, they were torn by dogs and perished, or were nailed to crosses, or were doomed to the flames and burnt, to serve as nightly illumination, when daylight had expired. Nero offered his gardens for the spectacle."

How true were the words of Paul to the early Christians: "We must go through many hardships to enter the kingdom of God" (Acts 14:22).

Someone has said that these are God's "permitted contradictions" in our lives. However, there is a drastic difference between God's permissive will and His perfect will for our lives. We strayed from that *perfect* will when Adam chose to disobey God in the Garden.

As life hits us head-on we can respond with resentment, resignation, acceptance, or welcome. We are the living examples of our responses.

Resentment: It's Your Fault, God

If we are living self-centered lives and something happens to upset or disrupt our carefully laid plans, our natural tendency is to react with impatience and resentment. We tend to blame God when things go wrong and take credit for ourselves when things seem to be going right. Reacting resentfully can become a way of life with us, and the result is not very attractive.

Resentment can strangle a human being. The Bible says, "Resentment kills a fool, and envy slays the simple" (Job 5:2).

How does resentment develop? It develops within the climate of resistance to God's will for our lives. Christians who are strong in faith grow as they accept whatever God allows to enter their lives. They bow to His good and perfect will and become more mature. In a true sense Christian character is growth, not a gift.

Alexander Maclaren, a distinguished Manchester preacher (1826–1910), wrote, "What disturbs us in this world is not trouble, but our opposition to trouble. The true source of all that frets and irritates and wears away our lives is not in external things but in the resistance of our wills to the will of God expressed by eternal things."

To resent and resist God's disciplining hand is to miss one of the greatest spiritual blessings we Christians can enjoy this side of heaven.

Whatever it is—aggravations, trouble, adversity, irritations, opposition—we haven't "learned Christ" until we have discovered that God's grace is sufficient for every test. Some unknown poet asks:

> If all my years were summer, could I know
>> what my Lord means by His "made white as snow"?
> If all my days were sunny, could I say,
>> "In His fair land He wipes all tears away"?
> If I were never weary, could I keep
>> close to my heart, "He gives His loved one sleep"?
> Were no griefs mine, might I not come to deem
>> the eternal life but a baseless dream?
> My winter, and my tears, and my weariness,
>> even my griefs may be His way to bless.
> I call them ills, yet they can surely be
>> nothing but love that shows my Lord to me.

Though Job suffered as few men have, he never lost sight of God's presence with him in the midst of suffering. He emerged victorious on the other side of sorrow and testing because he never allowed resentment to cloud his relationship with God.

The attitude which can overcome resentment is expressed by the writer to the Hebrews: "No discipline seems pleasant at the time, but painful. Later on, however, it produces a harvest of righteousness and peace for those who have been trained by it" (12:11).

Resentment is one response to life's trials and afflictions, and it leaves us with an embittered personality. There is another response which takes on an appearance of piety.

Resignation: Greeting Life with a Sigh

A whole genre of religious literature has developed around this type of "spiritual" attitude. In fact, most Christians find themselves in this category at some time. Somehow we feel there is something pious in resigning ourselves to hard knocks. Resignation is not distinctly a Christian virtue. We could learn from pagan writers, like the Stoics of ancient Greece, about accepting calamity with resignation. Often it's the easy way out, a sort of fatalism or painkiller—anesthesia where there should be action.

Authentic Christian victory does not lie along the path of mere resignation. Instead, the growing Christian sees, as Job did, that though God may wound us (or allow us to be wounded), "his hands also heal" (Job 5:18).

I am so glad King David did not live on a perpetual "high." Think of the Psalms we would have missed in that case. Throughout his writings he shows a side of his nature that intrigues and inspires us. Rather than *resign* himself to suffering, he said things like: "Why are you downcast, O my soul? Why so disturbed within me?" (Ps. 42:5).

How did he respond to these rhetorical questions? He went on, "Put your hope in God, for I will yet praise him, my Savior and my God" (vv.5,6). He continues to reason within himself, "By day the Lord directs his love, at night his song is with me—a prayer to the God of my life. I say to God my Rock, 'Why have you forgotten me? . . .' Why are you downcast, O my soul? Why so disturbed within me?" He answers himself triumphantly, "Put your hope in God, for I will yet praise him, my Savior and my God" (vv.8–11).

David refused to resign himself to the defeats that sometimes threatened to flatten him. More than once, in his personal as well as his public life, he seemed to be "down for the count"—but he always looked beyond the obstacle or problem to God Himself. "I lift up my eyes to the hills—where does my help come from? My help comes from the Lord, the Maker of heaven and earth" (Ps. 121:1,2). However sad, puzzled or discouraged David reveals himself to be in some Psalms, he always ends on a note of hope or confidence in God.

As we have already pointed out, sorrow, difficulties, suffering, and even persecution come, in some form or another, to every Christian's life. We don't have a magic shield to protect us from problems. But mere resignation can lead to a spirit of despondency. In the end it is our attitude that counts—our attitude toward ourselves and toward God. We can turn burdens into blessings, or we can let those burdens bury us.

Acceptance: Taking Advantage of Adversity

Sometimes our burdens seem too large for anyone to handle.

Jesus has a great invitation for us: *"Come* to me, all you who are weary and burdened, and I will give you rest. *Take* my yoke upon you and *learn* from me, for I am gentle and humble in heart, and you will find rest for your souls. For my yoke is easy and my burden is light" (Matt. 11:28–30, italics mine).

Come. Take. Learn. What powerful words! They contain an invitation to accept and take advantage of our burdens and problems.

The Irish orator, writer, and statesman, Edmund Burke (1729–1797), said, "Our antagonist is our helper. He that wrestles with us strengthens our muscles and sharpens our skills."

A muscle becomes atrophied if it is unused. To reach optimum strength, a muscle must push against something. To reach the greatest heights as an individual, a person must learn how to take advantage of a difficulty.

I think of the black people in America and how for many years they were given second-class status as citizens. But, in spite of their extreme disadvantages, many blacks have taken advantage of their difficulties to reach for their optimum potential. As a result of their working and striving for recognition, we have many outstanding black entertainers— athletes, singers, actors. Other blacks, as well, have achieved great heights because they have found in adversity what we in privilege and affluency have often missed.

The pearl is another example of greatness coming out of adversity. Where does this beautiful jewel come from? It begins as an irritating grain of sand, which somehow has made its way between the folds of the oyster shell. The pearl emerges as the result of the oyster's reaction to the irritant. Someone has said, "A pearl is an oyster that has been wounded."

Comfort and prosperity have never enriched the world as adversity has done. Out of pain and problems have come the sweetest songs, the most poignant poems, the most gripping stories. Out of suffering and tears have come the greatest spirits and the most blessed lives.

J. R. Miller wrote: "Many of us find life hard and full of pain. We cannot avoid these things; but we should not allow the harsh experiences to deaden our sensibilities, or make us stoical or sour. The true problem of living is to keep our hearts sweet and gentle in the hardest conditions and experiences."

Our oldest daughter married a Swiss. They have six children and usually spend their summers in Switzerland and their winters in America. Sometimes when we visit them in Switzerland we take the children and go high up in the Alps on chair lifts. We cross over miles of land, looking down below at some of the most beautiful flowers to be found anywhere in the world. These flowers have survived the heavy snows of winter. The burdens of ice, snow, and winter storms have added to their luster, beauty, and growth. It is hard to believe that just a few weeks earlier these flowers were buried under many feet of snow. Our burdens can have the same effect on our lives.

As Christians face the winds of adversity and the storms of trouble, they rise like the skylark. They are like the trees that survive the storm because their roots are driven deep. They are like the trees that grow on our mountain ridges in North Carolina—trees battered by winds, yet, trees in which we find the strongest wood.

The pearl, the skylark, the flower, the trees—all these illustrate Job's words, "When he has tested me, I will come forth as gold" (23:10). The Christian who understands this aspect of God's nature can find comfort in his suffering. Just as a disciplined child is a happy child, the Bible says, "Blessed is the man whom God corrects; so do not despise the discipline of the Almighty. For he wounds, but he also binds up; he injures, but his hands also heal" (Job 5:17,18).

When our hearts are surrendered totally to the will of God,

then we delight in seeing Him use us in any way He desires. Our plans and desires begin to agree with His and we accept His direction in our lives. Our sense of joy, satisfaction, and fulfillment in life increases, no matter what the circumstances, if we are in the center of God's will.

Welcome Suffering: Joy in Spite of the Furnace

Resentment or resignation are not the answer to the problem of suffering. And there is another step beyond acceptance. *It is accepting with joy.* We need to listen to the words of James: "Consider it pure joy, my brothers, whenever you face trials of many kinds, because you know that the testing of your faith develops perseverance. Perseverance must finish its work so that you may be mature and complete, not lacking anything" (1:2–4).

The Christian life is a joyful life. Christianity was never meant to be something to make people miserable. The ministry of Jesus Christ was one of joy. The Bible teaches that a life of inward rest and outward victory is a Christian's birthright.

"What a witness to the world Christians would be," wrote Amy Carmichael, "if only they were more evidently very happy people." Joy is one of the marks of a true believer. Miss Carmichael quotes Prebendary Webb-Peploe as having said: "'Joy is not gush: joy is not jolliness. Joy is simply perfect acquiescence in God's will, because the soul delights itself in God Himself.'"[2]

The ability to rejoice in any situation is a sign of spiritual maturity.

Christ told His disciples that they were not to regard it as a stroke of affliction when they were reviled and persecuted. Rather, they were to count it as a favor and a blessing. They were to "rejoice and be glad" when persecuted (Matt. 5:12). They were to be "more than conquerors" amid their privation (Rom. 8:37). They were to rejoice in their sufferings (Rom. 5:3).

---

2. Amy Carmichael, *Gold by Moonlight* (London: S.P.C.K., 1952), pp. 73–74.

Paul sang and shouted his way through trouble, his greatest victories arising out of his persecutions. To the Romans he wrote: "We also rejoice in our sufferings, because we know that suffering produces perseverance; . . . Who shall separate us from the love of Christ? Shall trouble or hardship or persecution . . .? Be joyful in hope, patient in affliction, faithful in prayer" (5:3; 8:35; 12:12).

When flogged and ordered not to speak any longer in the name of Jesus, Peter and John departed "rejoicing because they had been counted worthy of suffering disgrace for the Name. . . . they never stopped teaching and proclaiming the good news that Jesus is the Christ" (Acts 5:41,42).

In all ages Christians have found it possible to maintain the spirit of joy in the hour of trial. In circumstances that would have felled most men, they have so completely risen above their difficulties that they actually have used them to serve and glorify Christ.

The Christian's Secret of Joy

When Jesus Christ is the source of joy, there are no words that can describe it. It is a joy "inexpressible and glorious" (1 Pet. 1:8). Christ is the answer to the sadness and discouragement, the discord and division in our world.

Christ can take discouragement and despondency out of our lives. Optimism and cheerfulness are products of knowing Him.

The Bible says, "A cheerful heart is good medicine, but a crushed spirit dries up the bones" (Prov. 17:22).

If the heart has been attuned to God through faith in Christ, then its overflow will be joyous optimism and good cheer.

Out West an old sheepherder had a violin, but it was out of tune. He had no way of tuning it, so in desperation he wrote to one of the radio stations and asked them at a certain hour on a certain day to strike the tone "A." The officials of the station decided they would accommodate the old fellow, and on that particular day the true tone of "A" was broadcast. His fiddle was thus tuned, and once more his cabin echoed with joyful music.

We have to be tuned to God. We will never be free from discouragement and despondency until we know and walk with the very fountainhead of joy.

Christ Himself is the Christian's secret of joy: "Though you have not seen him, you love him; and even though you do not see him now, you believe in him and are filled with an inexpressible and glorious joy" (1 Pet. 1:8).

Sin: Barrier to Joy

As we have seen, but cannot repeat often enough, the Bible indicates that all the troubles of the world stem from the fact that men have broken the laws of God. "All have sinned and fall short of the glory of God" (Rom. 3:23).

There is a penalty for breaking God's law, and that penalty is banishment from His presence. How can anyone who is part of such a world know joy? There is a wall between that person and God.

However, the Scripture says that in Christ "we have redemption through his blood, the forgiveness of sins, in accordance with the riches of God's grace" (Eph. 1:7).

By the Cross Christ has broken down the barrier built by sin so that we may know the joy of God's salvation. The Bible says, "If we confess our sins, he is faithful and just and will forgive us our sins and purify us from all unrighteousness" (1 John 1:9).

Affliction can be a means of refining and purification. Many a life has come forth from the furnace of affliction as we have shown earlier (e.g., in chapters 6 and 9). Thousands of Christians have learned the secret of contentment and joy in trial. Some of the happiest Christians I have met have drunk the full cup of trial and misfortune. Some have been lifelong sufferers. They have had every reason to sigh and complain, being denied so many privileges and pleasures that they see others enjoy; yet they have found greater cause for gratitude and joy than many who are prosperous, vigorous, and strong.

A father was visiting his son at the university. As they were standing in the union quad on campus, suddenly a cheerful young man came riding up in an electric wheelchair. The son said, "Father, I want you to meet the happiest friend I have. He is a Christian." My friend was astounded to meet a very positive, joyful young man because his son's newfound friend had short stubs for arms and no legs.

While rewriting this chapter I visited an elderly man who had spent most of his life in China as a missionary. He has always enjoyed good health and has had an extraordinary physical strength that many admired. But it has been his deep dedication to Christ and the love between him and his wife that has made people love him. Now he has cancer in many parts of his body. I went to minister to him, but instead he ministered to me. There was about him a joy and radiance and happiness that I have rarely seen. He got up out of bed and walked me to the car when I left; then with a great smile and wave of his hand he said, "Keep on preaching the gospel. The older I get, the better Christ is to me."

We are not surprised that the early Christians rejoiced in spite of suffering, since they looked at it in the light of eternity. The nearer death, the nearer a life of eternal fellowship with Christ. When Ignatius was about to die for his faith in A.D. 110 he cried out, "Nearer the sword, then nearer to God. In company with wild beasts, in company with God."

The apostle Paul wrote: "Our present sufferings are not worth comparing with the glory that will be revealed in us" (Rom. 8:18). In my travels I have found that those who keep heaven in view remain serene and cheerful in the darkest day. If the glories of heaven were more real to us, if we lived less for material things and more for things eternal and spiritual, we would be less easily disturbed by this present life.

How Do You React?

How do you react as you approach your own armageddons, or perhaps the final Armageddon? Will pain drive you to God or drive you away from Him?

We can resent suffering, resign ourselves to it—or accept it with joy because we know that God is in control of our lives. The root word for rejoice means *extreme* joy, *hilarious* joy, *triumphant* joy. Amy Carmichael (1867–1951) wrote:

> Before the winds that blow do cease,
> Teach me to dwell within Thy calm:
> Before the pain has passed in peace,
> Give me, my God, to sing a psalm.
> Let me not lose the chance to prove
> The fullness of enabling love.[3]

When the Holy Spirit of God is having His way in my life, I will be able to sing this victorious song with Amy Carmichael. Though bedridden as a result of an accident some twenty years before her death, and in almost constant pain, she continued to minister through her devotional writings and poetry, staying at the heart of the Dohnavur Fellowship in India. Her keen insight and her refreshingly spiritual writings revealed the depth of her walk with Christ. She remains a striking example of a Christian whose physical suffering enabled her to reflect the character of Christ. She lived a life of rejoicing in the midst of tribulation. Her face radiated the love of Christ, and her life epitomized the saintly stature the surrendered Christian can reach if he reacts to suffering by rejoicing in it.

During those years of physical pain, Amy Carmichael wrote the many books that have blessed untold thousands around the world. Without the "blessing" of being confined to her bed, she might have been too busy to write.

There is a story about Martin Luther going through a period of depression and discouragement. For days his long face graced the family table and dampened the family's home life. One day his wife came to the breakfast table all dressed in black, as if she were going to a funeral service. When Martin asked her who had died, she replied, "Martin, the way you've been behaving lately, I thought God had died, so I came prepared to attend His funeral."

Her gentle but effective rebuke drove straight to Luther's heart, and as a result of that homely lesson the great Reformer resolved never again to allow worldly care, resentment, depression, discouragement, or frustration to defeat him. By God's grace, he vowed, he would submit his life to the Savior

---

3. Amy Carmichael, *Rose From Brier* (Fort Washington, PA: Christian Literature Crusade, 1973), p. 12.

and reflect His grace in a spirit of rejoicing, whatever came. With Paul he would shout, "Thanks be to God! He gives us the victory through our Lord Jesus Christ" (1 Cor. 15:57).

God gives us tough assignments in life and then asks us to be joyful about them. In his *Diary of the Sinai Campaign,* General Moshe Dayan writes: "Officers selected to command fighting units have been men whose natural reaction to a tough assignment was never 'But . . .' . . . They understood the full significance of my early warning order. Yet they did not shrink from its implications: rather they welcomed them."[4]

Rich Rewards

In these days of spiritual darkness and political upheaval, the forward-looking Christian remains optimistic and joyful, knowing that Christ must reign, and "if we endure, we will also reign with him" (2 Tim. 2:12).

For every man, woman, and child throughout the world who is suffering, our Lord has these words from the Sermon on the Mount: "Blessed are you when people insult you, persecute you and falsely say all kinds of evil against you because of me. Rejoice and be glad, because great is your reward in heaven, for in the same way they persecuted the prophets who were before you" (Matt. 5:11,12).

Perhaps in your particular circumstances you are undergoing psychological suffering which is just as real as physical suffering. It may be a suffering that you cannot express, even to your dearest friend—an inward, heartrending, heartbreaking suffering. In the midst of it all, there is the promise of victory. Christ has overcome the world, and you, by faith, can overcome the world through our Lord Jesus Christ (1 John 5:5).

There is a joy to be discovered in the midst of suffering. Sometimes we encounter it in our earthly pilgrimage. Once we acknowledge that possibility, we will be astounded at how possible it is to be "surprised by joy," as C. S. Lewis put it.

Billy Sunday described it well when he said, "If you have no

---

4. (New York: Harper & Row, 1966), pp. 32–33.

joy in your religion, there's a leak in your Christianity somewhere!"

Rejoice! The summons to rejoice is sounded no less than seventy times in the New Testament. There is a vast difference between pleasure and Christian joy. Pleasure depends on circumstances, but Christian joy is completely independent of health, money, or surroundings. When circumstances are against you, when every modern comfort is withdrawn, you may still experience the miracle of joy produced by the Holy Spirit who lives within.

I have been driven many times upon my knees by the overwhelming conviction that I had nowhere else to go. My own wisdom and that of all about me seemed insufficient for that day.[1]

ABRAHAM LINCOLN

11/

The Place of Prayer in Suffering

WHEN WE LOOK for the supreme model of a person devoted to prayer, we need only to consult the life of our Lord. Jesus was constantly in an attitude of prayer, and never more urgently than in the face of suffering.

The night when He was arrested, He was praying in the Garden of Gethsemane. He had taken His disciples with Him, but He Himself was so overwhelmed with what He knew lay before Him that He asked Peter, James, and John to stay and keep watch with Him. He Himself went still farther into the garden and fell on His face to the ground and prayed, "My Father, if it is possible, may this cup be taken from me. Yet not as I will, but as you will" (Matt. 26:39).

In those words Jesus taught us how to pray. Every time I pray for a sick person, a bereaved person, or a person in trouble, I always close by saying, "If it be Thy will." While it is God's will to save everyone who will repent of sin and receive His Son as Savior, it is not God's will to deliver us from every adversity. As we have already seen, suffering often strengthens us, and as Christians we cannot claim exemption from all life's ills.

---

1. Abraham Lincoln, *Harper's New Monthly Magazine* no. 182, vol. 31, (July 1865).

Prayer was as natural as breathing for our Lord, and it should be the same for us. If prayer is an integral part of our lives, when a crisis comes we have already prepared those lines of communication.

In the beginning man was fashioned to live a life of prayer in fellowship with God and in humble dependence upon Him. When we pray we are fulfilling God's purpose for our lives, realizing our spiritual potential. As someone has said, "Prayer is the highest use to which speech can be put."

The British author, William Ernest Henley, wrote the poem, "Invictus," which has been studied by high school students for generations and which expresses feelings that sound so noble:

> It matters not how strait the gate,
> How charged with punishments the scroll,
> I am the master of my fate:
> I am the captain of my soul.[2]

All this looks very brave on paper, but when death took Henley's six-year-old daughter, Margaret, he was heartbroken and began to realize that he was not the master of his fate. When she neared death, his bravado completely disappeared.

This kind of an attitude cannot be the stance of the Christian in any situation, particularly in the face of suffering. We are *not* the masters of our fate, either as individuals or as a nation. How can men boast that they control their own destiny when they cannot solve the problems of war, racism, poverty, sickness, or suffering?

No Freedom without God's Help

As we have already emphasized, the world is being carried along on a rushing torrent of events which are beyond man's control. Armageddon seems to be approaching in one form or another. However, there is one power available to change the course of events and to support us in the great crises of life, and that is the power of prayer by God-fearing men and women.

---

2. *A Treasury of Great Poems, English and American,* Louis Untermeyer, ed. (New York: Simon and Schuster, 1942, 1955), p. 985.

Adapting the words of Benjamin Franklin at the Constitutional Convention: It is probable that a nation cannot survive in freedom without the aid of Almighty God. Yet today we have reached the point where God is largely ignored, and we regard prayer in national life as no more than a venerated tradition. We have no sense of coming earnestly and expectantly to God; we simply use prayer as a formality.

Prayer Is Effective

From one end of the Bible to the other there is the record of those whose prayers have been answered—people who turned the tide of history by prayer, men who prayed fervently and God answered.

Elijah prayed when challenged by his enemies, and fire was sent from heaven to consume the offering on the altar he had built in the presence of God's enemies.

Elisha prayed, and the son of the Shunammite woman was raised from the dead.

David prayed, and some of his psalms could serve as "pattern prayers" for others who are going through difficulty or as examples of how to praise the Lord in the midst of trouble:

"Answer me when I call to you, O my righteous God. Give me relief from my distress; be merciful to me and hear my prayer" (Ps. 4:1).

"The Lord has heard my cry for mercy; the Lord accepts my prayer" (Ps. 6:9).

"In my distress I called to the Lord; I cried to my God for help. From his temple he heard my voice; my cry came before him, into his ears" (Ps. 18:6).

"O Lord my God, I called to you for help and you healed me" (Ps. 30:2).

"In you, O Lord, I have taken refuge; let me never be put to shame; deliver me in your righteousness. Turn your ear to me, come quickly to my rescue; be my rock of refuge, a strong fortress to save me" (Ps. 31:1,2).

Daniel prayed, and the secret of God was made known to him for the saving of his and his companions' lives, and the changing of the course of history.

Jesus prayed at the tomb of Lazarus, and the one who had

been dead for four days came forth. He prayed in the Garden of Gethsemane and found strength to endure His suffering.

The thief prayed on a cross, and Jesus assured him that on that same day he would be with Him in paradise.

The early church prayed, and Peter was miraculously released from prison.

Peter prayed, and Dorcas was raised to life to have added years of service for Jesus Christ.

When the disciples came to Jesus and asked, "Lord, teach us to pray," the Savior answered their request by giving them "The Lord's Prayer" as a model petition. The Lord's Prayer, however, was only the beginning of His teaching on this subject. In scores of passages Christ offered further guidance, and because He practiced what He preached, His whole life was a series of lessons on how prayer prevails in every aspect of life.

Christ's Example

One of the most amazing things in all the Scriptures is how much time Jesus spent in prayer. He had only three years of public ministry, yet He was never too hurried to spend hours in prayer. He prayed before every difficult task and at every crisis in His ministry. He prayed with regularity. We may be sure that never a day began or closed on which He did not hold communion with His Father.

How haphazardly and carelessly, by contrast, do we pray. Snatches of memorized verses are hastily spoken in the morning; then we say good-bye to God for the rest of the day, until we rush through a few closing petitions at night.

This is not the prayer program that Jesus exemplified. He prayed long and repeatedly. It is recorded that He spent one entire night in prayer to God (Luke 6:12).

The Scripture says, "Pray without ceasing" (1 Thess. 5:17, KJV). This should be the motto of every true follower of Jesus Christ. Never stop praying, no matter how dark and hopeless your case may seem. Jesus taught us that we should keep on praying and never give up (Luke 18:1).

A few months ago a woman wrote me that she had pleaded for ten years for the conversion of her husband, but that he was more hardened than ever. I advised her to continue to pray. Recently I heard from her again. She said her husband was gloriously and miraculously converted in the eleventh year of her praying. Suppose she had stopped after only ten years?

Our Lord frequently prayed alone, separating Himself from every earthly distraction. I would strongly urge you to select a place—a room or corner in your home, place of work, or in your yard or garden—where alone you can regularly meet God.

As we observe the prayer life of Jesus, we notice the earnestness with which He prayed. The New Testament records that in Gethsemane, in the intensity of His supplication, He fell to the ground and agonized with God until His sweat became "like drops of blood" (Luke 22:44). What an example of "prayer in suffering" He is—and how He proves the promise that those who are suffering need to look to God even more earnestly.

So many are the lessons Jesus taught us about prayer that I cannot present them all in one chapter. However, one that we should especially remember during these days of prejudice, hate, and hostility is this. He tells us to "pray for those who persecute you" (Matt. 5:44). We are to plead for our enemies, asking God to lead them to Christ and for His sake to forgive them. Even those who persecute us are to be the objects of our prayers.

Jesus reinforced this teaching by His own example, as we have seen. In the first words He uttered from the cross after the nails had been hammered through His hands and feet, He began to intercede for His crucifiers, saying, "Father, forgive them, for they do not know what they are doing" (Luke 23:34). I have often thought that we will see the men who nailed Jesus to the cross in heaven because of His prayer. No prayer that Jesus ever prayed to the Father went unanswered.

With God nothing is impossible. No task is too arduous, no problem too difficult, no burden is too heavy for His love. The future with all its uncertainties is fully known to Him, though hidden from us.

He understands how much affliction and sorrow you need in order that your soul may be purified and preserved for eternity. Turn to Him, and you can say with Job, "He knows the way that I take; when he has tested me, I will come forth as gold" (Job 23:10).

Jesus considered prayer more important than food, for the Bible says that hours before breakfast, "Very early in the morning, while it was still dark, Jesus got up, left the house and went off to a solitary place, where he prayed" (Mark 1:35).

To the Son of God, prayer was more important than the assembling and the healing of great throngs. The Bible says, "Crowds of people came to hear him and to be healed of their sicknesses. But Jesus often withdrew to lonely places and prayed" (Luke 5:15,16).

The precious hours of fellowship with His heavenly Father meant much more to our Savior than sleep, for the Bible says, "Jesus went out into the hills to pray, and spent the night praying to God" (Luke 6:12).

He prayed at funerals, and the dead were raised. He prayed over the five loaves and two fishes, and fed a multitude with a little boy's lunch. In the contemplation of His imminent suffering on Calvary's cross He prayed, "Not my will, but yours" (Luke 22:42), and a way was made whereby sinful man might approach a holy God.

Prayer, in the true sense, is not a futile cry of desperation born of fear and frustration. Many people pray only when they are under great stress, or in danger, or facing some crisis. I have been in airplanes when an engine died; then people started praying. I have flown through bad thunderstorms when people who may never have thought to pray before were praying all around me. I have talked to soldiers who told me that they never prayed until they were in the midst of battle. There seems to be an instinct in man to pray in times of danger.

We know "there are few atheists in foxholes," but that kind of Christianity fails to reach into our everyday lives, and it is too shallow to be genuine.

Christian teachers down through the ages have urged the prominence that prayer should have in the lives of believers. Some anonymous wise man has said, "If Christians spent as much time praying as they do grumbling, they would soon have nothing to grumble about."

Here are some thoughts on prayer.

In the morning, prayer is the key that opens to us the

treasures of God's mercies and blessings; in the evening, it is the key that shuts us up under His protection and safeguard.

"God's way of answering the Christian's prayer for more patience, experience, hope and love is often to put him into the furnace of affliction," *Richard Cecil* (1748–1810).

"Our prayer and God's mercy are like two buckets in a well; while the one ascends, the other descends," *Mark Hopkins,* American educator (1802–1887).

My longtime friend, that great humanitarian missionary and man of prayer, *Frank C. Laubach,* said, "Prayer at its highest is a two-way conversation—and for me the most important is listening to God's replies."

"Satan trembles when he sees the weakest saint upon his knees," *William Cowper* (1731–1800).

If there are any tears shed in heaven, they will be over the fact that we prayed so little.

Heaven is full of answers to prayer for which no one ever bothered to ask!

The Power and Privilege of Prayer

In our modern age we have learned to harness the power of the mighty Niagara and turn its force to beneficial use. We have learned to hold steam captive in boilers and release its tremendous energy to turn our machines and pull our trains. We have learned to contain gasoline vapors in a cylinder and explode them at the appointed second to move our automobiles and trucks along our highways. We have even discovered the secret of releasing energy in the atom, which is capable of lighting cities, operating great industries, or of destroying entire cities and civilizations.

But very few of us have learned how to fully develop the power of prayer. *We have not yet learned that a man is more powerful when he is at prayer than when he is in control of the most powerful military weapons we have ever developed.*

Effectual prayer is offered in faith. Jesus said, "I tell you, whatever you ask for in prayer, believe that you have received it, and it will be yours" (Mark 11:24). James wrote: "If any of you lacks wisdom, he should ask God, who gives generously to all without finding fault, and it will be given to him. But when he asks, he must believe and not doubt, because he who doubts is like a wave of the sea, blown and tossed by the wind" (James 1:5,6). If our prayers are aimless, meaningless, and mingled with doubt, they will be unanswered. Prayer is more than a wish turned heavenward: it is the voice of faith directed Godward.

What a privilege is yours—the privilege of prayer! In the light of coming events, examine your heart, re-consecrate your life, yield yourself to God unreservedly, for only those who pray through a clean heart will be heard of Him. The Bible says, "The prayer of a righteous man is powerful and effective" (James 5:16).

We are to pray not only for our own needs but for the needs of others. We are to pray in times of adversity, lest we become faithless and unbelieving. We are to pray in times of prosperity, lest we become boastful and proud. We are to pray in times of danger, lest we become fearful and doubting. We need to pray in times of security, lest we become careless and self-sufficient.

"More things are wrought by prayer than this world dreams of." Tennyson's well-known words are no mere cliché. They state a sober truth. Bible teaching, church history, Christian experience, all confirm that prayer *does* work. But as we relate this matter of prayer specifically to the subject of suffering, we need to keep in mind several things which we have already stated and which we now summarize.

For one thing, we must always remember that prayer does not work automatically, nor is it a piece of spiritual magic. It's not like pressing an electric button and expecting an immediate response. We can't manipulate God or dictate to Him. He is sovereign, and we must recognize His sovereign rights.

This means, as we have stressed all along, that our prayers are subject to His will. And we should be glad of that. It takes the burden off ourselves and places it on the Lord. To say "Thy will be done" is not a sigh, but a song because His will is always what is best—both for us and those for whom we pray. As Dante said, "in His will is our peace." As believers we cannot find true peace outside the will of God.

Again, we may be sure that God is true to His Word and answers all sincere prayer offered in the name of the Lord

Jesus Christ. But His answer is not always the same. As is so often pointed out, His answer may not necessarily be "Yes." It may be "No"—or it may be "Wait." If it is "No" or "Wait" we have no right to say that God has not answered our prayer. It simply means that the answer is different from what we expected. We must get rid of the idea that if only we pray hard and long enough God will always give us what we ask for in the end.

As we have seen, when we pray for help in trouble or for healing in sickness or for deliverance in persecution, God may not give us what we ask for, for that may not be His wise and loving will for us. But He *will* answer our prayer in His own way. He will not let us down in our hour of need. He will give us the patience, courage and strength to endure our suffering, the ability to rise above it, and the assurance of His presence in all that we are called to pass through.

In any case, let us never forget that prayer is not just *asking* God for things. It's far bigger and better than that. At its deepest level, prayer is *fellowship with God:* enjoying His company, waiting upon His will, thanking Him for His mercies, committing our lives to Him, talking to Him about other people as well as ourselves, and listening in the silence for what He has to say to us.

This is what makes prayer so real and precious a thing, especially in times of stress and strain. When we come to the end of ourselves, we come to the beginning of God. As it has been said, our little things are all big to God's love; our big things are all small to His power.

You are denying yourself a marvelous privilege if you don't pray. The path of prayer is always open, whatever your need. Take it to the Lord in prayer!

*In times of affliction we commonly
meet with the sweetest experiences
of the love of God.[1]*

JOHN BUNYAN

12/

*Promises for Those
Who Suffer*

THE BIBLE IS God's book of promises, and, unlike the
books of men, it does not change or get out of date. In Titus
1:2 Paul says we have "a faith and knowledge resting on the
hope of eternal life, which God, *who does not lie,* promised
before the beginning of time" (italics mine). I have been
preaching the Bible and proclaiming the Word of God for
many years (our international radio broadcast, "The Hour of
Decision," began on November 5, 1950, and has continued
weekly without a break ever since), and the message I have
been preaching throughout that time is basically the same—
because *God does not lie!*

In the intervening years many changes have taken place in
our world. In fact, it is no longer the same world; it is totally
different. We are now preaching to a new generation of
people—people who have grown up in a new society and are
challenged by new ideas. But one thing is certain. *God has not
changed.* He said, "I the Lord do not change" (Mal. 3:6). This
is an immeasurable comfort to the believer in times of

---

1. John Bunyan, *The Complete Works of John Bunyan,* Henry Stebbing, ed., vol. 4
(London: Virtue & Yorston, n.d.), p. 494.

suffering. God is unchanging in His compassion and care for His afflicted children.

John Bunyan tells us, "Afflictions are governed by God, both as to time, number, nature, and measure. Our times, and our conditions in these times, are in the hand of God, yea, and so are our souls and bodies, to be kept and preserved from the evil while the rod of God is upon us." God is interested in and concerned about every aspect of our lives—physical, mental, emotional and spiritual. The Bible makes it clear that nothing that concerns us is beneath *His* concern. And that truth is what we are going to explore together in this chapter.

Because the Bible is so full of promises, we cannot possibly cover all of them in a chapter. Indeed, I would hesitate to try to deal with all the promises of the Bible within the scope of one book, although Dr. Herbert Lockyer has done a masterful job of doing just that in his book *All the Promises of the Bible* (Grand Rapids, Zondervan, 1962). Estimates as to the number of promises in the Bible range all the way from 8,000 to 30,000.

There are many different ways in which we could approach the subject. A rather obvious one would be to divide the promises according to their location in the Bible, whether they appear in the Old or New Testament. Indeed, both parts of the Bible are full of promises, as we will see later in this chapter. A whole book could be written, for example, just on the promises that appear in the Psalms.

Another approach would be to list the promises according to whether they are "general" or "specific." Many of the promises *are* of a general nature, while many others deal with specific areas of life. In this chapter, however, we are going to limit our discussion and choice of Scriptures to those which deal directly with the question of suffering as it affects the life of the Christian.

First of all, let us look at some Old Testament promises directed to those who undergo suffering and persecution, and then we will turn to the New Testament promises.

God Is Our Shield

Of the Israeli tribe of Benjamin, Moses said, "Let the beloved of the Lord rest secure in him, for *he shields him all day long,* and the one the Lord loves rests between his shoulders" (Deut. 33:12, italics mine).

Every persecuted Christian can apply these words to himself. All God's children are beloved of Him and are equally safe in His constant care. The feeblest Christian is as safe in God's care as the oldest and most experienced saint. The Lord Himself covers them the whole day long. As the songwriter put it,

> Under His wings, under His wings,
> Who from His love can sever?
> Under His wings my soul shall abide,
> Safely abide forever.[2]

The figure here is of a parent eagle protecting its offspring by sheltering it under its wings.

What an illustration of the way God cares for His children! Psalm 91:4 amplifies this picture: "He will cover you with his feathers, and under his wings you will find refuge; his faithfulness will be your shield and rampart."

God Is Our Refuge

"God is our refuge and strength, an ever present help in trouble" (Ps. 46:1). The picture here is not of one who huddles passive and panic-stricken behind a protective wall or under a sheltering roof. Rather it is a picture of one actively involved in the marketplace of life, for the psalmist says that God is not only a refuge, but he is "an *ever present* help in trouble" (italics mine). Our God is a God for the arena of life. He goes *with* His people into the scene of suffering and onto the platform of pain, not necessarily to deliver them *from* their trouble but to sustain them in the midst of it.

In Psalm 91:15 God promises, "He will call upon me, and I will answer him; I will be with him in trouble." Again, Scripture says, "Trust in him at all times, O people; pour out your hearts to him, for God is our refuge" (Ps. 62:8).

In another place the psalmist says, "It is time for you to act, O Lord" (119:126). J. R. Stam tells of a Chinese girl who did

---

2. William O. Cushing and Ira D. Sankey, "Under His Wings," in *Hymns for the Family of God* (Nashville: Paragon Associates, 1976), p. 412.

housework for John and Betty Stam, missionaries in China who were killed for their faith many years ago. She came to the Lord through their witness. One day, in a sudden turn of events, the maid found herself in rather difficult circumstances and ran off to her bedroom to pray. The Stams were deeply touched as they overheard her impassioned prayer which closed with the words, "Now's your chance, Lord! Now's your chance!" The psalmist's urgent thought was put into practice by an unlearned Chinese girl. She can be a picture of all of us as we come helplessly into the presence of our heavenly Father to seek His help.

God *is* a very present help in trouble, but we sometimes allow bitterness to keep Him at a distance and thus we miss His help.

The young Irish immigrant, Joseph Scriven (1820–1886) was deeply in love with a young woman, and their marriage plans had been made. Not long before their wedding day, however, she was drowned. For months Scriven was bitter, in utter despair. At last he turned to Christ, and through His grace, he found peace and comfort. Out of this experience he wrote the familiar hymn which has brought consolation to millions of aching hearts: "What a Friend we have in Jesus, All our sins and griefs to bear!"

Sometimes our way lies in the sunlight. It was thus for Joseph Scriven as he approached his wedding day. But like him, we may find that our path also leads through the dark shadows of loss, disappointment, and sorrow. At times like this it is within our power to turn our sufferings into occasions for a firmer grasp of God, and make them channels through which a surer and brighter hope may flow into our souls.

Business losses, pensions that don't pay the bills, loss of work, inflation, the sickness that lays us low, the sorrows that rob our homes of their light, children who rebel—all turned into blessings for those who by them become less attached to the earth and more attached to God.

Trouble will not hurt us unless it does what many of us too often allow it to do—harden us, making us sour, bitter and skeptical. The trouble we bear trustfully brings to us a fresh vision of God, and, as a result, we discover a new outlook on life.

If we make our sorrow and trouble an occasion for learning more of God's love and of His power to aid and bless, then it will teach us to have a firmer confidence in His providence; and as a result of this, the brightness of His love will fill our lives.

Trust with a childlike dependence on God, and no trouble can destroy you. Even in that last dark hour of death, when your flesh and your heart fail, you will be able to depend in peace upon Him who "is the strength of my heart and my portion forever" (Ps. 73:26).

God Is Our Strength

In Psalm 28:7 David says, "The Lord is my strength."

Primitive man believed that if one ate the flesh of a strong animal he would acquire the strength of that animal. We do get strength from meat—physical strength. But we need spiritual strength as well as physical strength. God is the soul's meat and drink. Feed upon Him, His Word, His truth, and you will be strong in the Lord and in the power of His might.

When tempted by the devil in the wilderness Jesus said, "Man does not live on bread alone, but on every word that comes from the mouth of God" (Matt. 4:4).

My wife is a great believer in vitamins. She takes several a day and urges me to do the same. Every time I sneeze she says, "Get the vitamin C!" If I cut my hand she says, "Rub some vitamin E on it." We hear today much about vitamins and foods enriched with vitamins, and the strength-giving value of these foods. It is well to give attention to this. We need to keep ourselves physically fit. But we also need to keep ourselves spiritually fit. That calls for spiritual vitamins, and to get these we must feed our souls on food enriched with spiritual truth.

In this world we are beset by many temptations and troubles. We are constantly under strain and stress. We need to draw on a source of strength above and beyond ourselves. God is that source.

As we look to God and trust in Him, as we open our hearts to Him, He will give us all the strength we have the capacity to receive. We shouldn't think about ourselves and how weak we are. Instead, we should think about God and how strong He is, focusing our attention on His available strength and waiting on Him in prayer.

"Those who hope in the Lord will renew their strength. They will soar on wings like eagles; they will run and not grow weary, they will walk and not be faint" (Isa. 40:31). This was Isaiah's way of expressing his belief in God's strengthening power.

With God as our strength, we can go out into the world with gladness in our hearts and a song of victory upon our lips. "The Lord is my strength and my shield; my heart trusts in him, and I am helped. My heart leaps for joy and I will give thanks to him in song" (Ps. 28:7).

An old translation of Psalm 68:28 has something to add to our understanding at this point: "The Lord hath sent strength for thee." The Lord is the source of that primary strength of character which makes it possible for us to surmount the suffering which life hands out to us. Paul prays for his readers that the Lord may "strengthen you with power through his Spirit in your inner being" (Eph. 3:16). The strength so imparted is continuous and exhaustless. As Moses told the children of Israel in Deuteronomy 33:25, "your strength will equal your days." This promise includes strength for all areas of life—physical, mental, and spiritual. God promises strength to enable us to survive suffering of whatever kind.

"The Lord is our strength" *to go on*. He is our source of strength for the daily grind. It is He who adds zest to our days and puts a spring in our step. Without Him the daily round would become tiresome and tedious, depressing and deadening, a drudgery to be endured rather than enjoyed.

I have met many people who are bored to death working in factories. They do exactly the same thing day after day, until much of their life seems to be absolutely meaningless and they feel they are getting nowhere. However, I have met others, who have accepted Christ and are tackling the same sort of tasks, and the day-to-day boredom has turned into a meaningful existence. They now have a purpose. Their faithfulness, whether it is as an executive or worker, glorifies God.

I was recently in a socialist country in Eastern Europe. One of the leaders of this country told me that they were finding

Christians to be the best and most faithful workers, the reason being they were no longer just "existing": they were living for God. Their faithfulness at a workbench had meaning in God's overall plan for their lives.

He is "my strength" *to go up*. The psalmist says, "By my God have I leaped over a wall" (Ps. 18:29, KJV). The obstacles before me would be mountains of difficulty if He did not step in and supply strength for the climb.

We live in the mountains of North Carolina. I have climbed many mountains. My wife and I almost daily took our children on mountain climbs when they were younger. We learned that we had to teach them to climb very small hills before they could manage a major mountain. After we have come to Christ, God may start us out on a small hill before He asks us to climb a mountain. However, whatever our need, He has promised that His power is available. Without it we would be unable to make the trip—let alone climb the steep places of pain and stress.

The Lord is also "my strength" *to go down*. Going down is often more difficult than going up.

One summer my wife and I were in Switzerland visiting our grandchildren. They took us to a very high mountain by cable car and then suggested that some of us walk down to a little restaurant below. It was only about a mile. But it was almost straight down. I got down all right, but my legs ached for nearly a week!

To go down into the Valley of Humiliation (as Bunyan called it), or into "the valley of the shadow of death," would be impossible without Him. Indeed, my heart would grow faint with fear and I would be gasping for breath were it not for the wonderful companion by my side, the Lord Jesus Christ.

Here is another point we don't often consider: the Lord is "my strength" simply to *sit still*. "Be still, and know that I am God" (Ps. 46:10). "I wait for the Lord, my soul waits, and in his word I put my hope" (Ps. 130:5). Our natural desire is to be doing something; but there are times in our lives when it is wiser to wait and just be still.

"The Lord is my strength!" Our sufficiency is of God, as Paul says—or as the modern version puts it, "Not that we are competent to claim anything for ourselves, but our competence comes from God" (2 Cor. 3:5).

God Is Our Shepherd

The wonderful picture of God as our Shepherd is found in many places in the Old Testament. One of the Psalms begins, "Hear us, O Shepherd of Israel, you who lead Joseph like a flock" (Ps. 80:1). It's great to think that the Everlasting God, the Almighty Creator, condescends to be the Shepherd of His people.

David makes the relationship a personal one in the best known of all Psalms. "The Lord is *my* shepherd," he cries exultantly, "I shall lack nothing" (Ps. 23:1, italics mine). The rest of the Psalm tells us what we shall not lack. It speaks of the shepherd's provision as He leads us to the green pastures, His guidance along the paths of righteousness (that means the right paths), His presence with us in the dark valley. No wonder David testifies, "My cup overflows" (v.5)—such are God's boundless blessings.

Isaiah adds a further touch to the picture when he says, "He tends his flock like a shepherd: He gathers the lambs in his arms and carries them close to his heart" (Isa. 40:11). The figure here indicates the tender care with which the Lord supports His people on their journey and the strong love with which He enfolds them.

In the New Testament Jesus uses this same figure and applies it to Himself. He says, "I am the good shepherd. The good shepherd lays down his life for the sheep. The hired hand is not the shepherd who owns the sheep. So when he sees the wolf coming, he abandons the sheep and runs away. Then the wolf attacks the flock and scatters it. . . . I am the good shepherd; I know my sheep and my sheep know me" (John 10:11–14).

Note four things about Jesus the Good Shepherd. He *owns* the sheep: they belong to Him. He *guards* the sheep: He never abandons them when danger is near. He *knows* the sheep, knows them each by name and leads them out (see v.3). And He *lays down His life* for the sheep, such is the measure of His love.

How thankful we should be, weak, wandering, and foolish as we are, that we have such a shepherd. Let's learn to keep close to Him, to listen to His voice, and follow Him. This is especially important in times of spiritual peril. Jesus tells us not to be misled by the voice of strangers (v.5), and there are many strange voices being heard in the religious world of our day. Don't be deceived by false teachers. Jesus is the Good Shepherd: trust Him. And Jesus is the door of salvation: enter by that door and you will find the full and abundant life He came to bring (vv.7–10).

God's Superabundant Provision for His Children

To encourage his fellow Christians with the reality of *God's interest* in and provision for them, the apostle Paul, in Ephesians 3:16–21, writes:

> I pray that out of his glorious riches he may strengthen you with power through his Spirit in your inner being, so that Christ may dwell in your hearts through faith. And I pray that you, being rooted and established in love, may have power, . . .
>
> Now to him who is able to do immeasurably more [KJV— "exceedingly abundantly"] than all we ask or imagine, according to his power that is at work within us, to him be glory in the church and in Christ Jesus throughout all generations, for ever and ever! Amen.

The phrase "exceedingly abundantly" is so thrilling and great that it is beyond our understanding or explanation. It reminds me of a new well that we have dug at our home. We reached one layer of water at 100 feet and another layer of water at 300 feet, then another at 600 feet. We asked the well diggers how much water they reckoned there was. They said there was no way to compute it, but that it would last forever. There is enough water in the well to furnish an entire town.

Recently I read about an oil man in Texas who was quoted as saying that even with the latest computers, he could not possibly compute how much oil reserves he himself controlled. He said, "We may come close, but we cannot be accurate." There are those who believe that America has plenty of oil and that we have enough coal to last over 600 years.

Computers are practically running our lives. Everything is now calculated by computers. But there is one thing that our most modern computers cannot measure and that is God's inexhaustible power which He has made available to us as a resource for our lives.

God's Presence Is Promised

James writes, "Come near to God and he will come near to you" (4:8). What a blessed promise and provision this is! It means that each of us can come close to God, with the assurance that He will come close to us—so close that we become conscious of an intimate, personal relationship with Him.

This is the greatest experience we can know, to have this sense of a personal relationship between God and ourselves. The conception is filled with rich meaning.

Every Christian life is closely bound up with the life of God because in Him we live and move and have our being. He breathed into us the breath of life. He has put something within us that is like unto Himself, something capable of developing into the rich quality of Christlike character.

Because God is the giver and source of our life, He has a legitimate claim upon our lives. He is our Father, and He has the right to expect us to be loyal and loving children. Because I am His child, He longs to have a fellowship with me.

The story of the prodigal son is a revelation of God's desire for human fellowship. He yearns over His children who have wandered far from Him and longs for them to come home and be near to Him.

All through the Bible we see God's patience and perseverance as He pursues misguided and obstinate men and women—men and women who were born to a high destiny as His sons and daughters, but who strayed from His side. From Genesis to Revelation God is constantly saying to such, "Return to me, and I will return to you."

Incredible as it may seem, God wants our companionship. He wants to have us close to Him. He wants to be a father to us, to shield us, to protect us, to counsel us, and to guide us in our way through life.

When we become Christians we can say "Our Father," for those who receive Christ have the right to become children of God (John 1:12). So then we can look to God as our Father. We are to put our trust in Him and come to know Him in the close, intimate companionship of father and child. We can have a personal sense of His love for us and His interest in us, for He is concerned about us as a father is concerned for his children.

As Peter Marshall once put it, "God will not permit any troubles to come upon us, unless he has a specific plan by which great blessing can come out of the difficulty."

It is through the suffering, the tests and trials of life, that we can draw near God. A. B. Simpson once heard a man say something that he never forgot. "When God tests you, it is a good time for you to test Him by putting His promises to the proof, and claiming from Him just as much as your trials have rendered necessary."

There are two ways of getting out of a trial. One is to simply try to get rid of the trial, and be thankful when it is over. The other is to recognize the trial as a challenge from God to claim a larger blessing than we have ever had.

God Will Supply All Your Needs

Paul told the Philippians, "My God will meet all your needs according to his glorious riches in Christ Jesus" (4:19). What a promise this is for the Christian! The source is God—"my God," the apostle calls Him. The supply is exhaustless— "according to his glorious riches." And the Savior is the channel through whom these riches come to us. The equation is totally in my favor. *My* needs are balanced over against *His* riches. There is no way I could improve upon that arrangement. No matter what my need, He is more than able to meet it. We are not to treat God as the anonymous writer puts it: "Some people treat God like they do a lawyer; they go to Him only when they are in trouble."

I find that I need Christ just as much, and sometimes more, in my more exalted hours as I do in the times of difficulties, troubles, and adversity. Many times we make the mistake of thinking that Christ's help is needed only for sickrooms or in times of overwhelming sorrow and suffering. This is not true. Jesus wishes to enter into every mood and every moment of our lives. He went to the wedding at Cana as well as to the home of Mary and Martha when Lazarus died. He wept with those who wept and rejoiced with those who rejoiced. Someone has said, "There are just as many stars in the sky at noon as at midnight, although we cannot see them in the sun's glare."

I seriously doubt if we will ever understand our trials and adversities until we are safely in heaven. Then when we look back we are going to be absolutely amazed at how God took care of us and blessed us even in the storms of life. We face dangers every day of which we are not even aware. Often God intervenes in our behalf through the use of His marvelous angels. I do not believe that anything happens to an obedient Christian by accident. It is all in God's purpose. "We know that in all things God works for the good of those who love him, who have been called according to his purpose" (Rom. 8:28).

The apostle Paul again said, "All this is for your benefit, so that the grace that is reaching more and more people may cause thanksgiving to overflow to the glory of God. Therefore we do not lose heart. Though outwardly we are wasting away, yet inwardly we are being renewed day by day. For our light and momentary troubles are achieving for us an eternal glory that far outweighs them all" (2 Cor. 4:15–17). He again wrote to the Corinthians, "All things are yours, whether . . . the world or life or death or the present or the future—all are yours" (1 Cor. 3:21,22).

God's Grace Is Sufficient

Out of his deep experience of physical suffering, his "thorn in the flesh," as he called it, Paul could write to the Corinthians, "He [God] said to me, 'My grace is sufficient for you, for my power is made perfect in weakness.'" He then went on to say, "Therefore I will boast all the more gladly about my weaknesses, so that Christ's power may rest on me" (2 Cor. 12:9). What a strange and unusual attitude toward suffering these words reveal! At first glance it reminds me of the man who was banging his head against the wall of his hospital room, and when the doctor asked him why he was doing it, he replied, "Because it feels so good when I stop!"

That wasn't what Paul was saying here. A word from the great "prince of preachers," Charles Haddon Spurgeon (1834–1892), helps me better to grasp what Paul meant:

> The other evening I was riding home after a heavy day's work. I felt very wearied, and sore depressed, when swiftly, and suddenly as a lightning flash, that text came to me, "My grace is sufficient for thee." I reached home and looked it up in the original, and at last it came to me in this way, *"MY grace is sufficient for thee";* and I said, "I should think it is, Lord," and burst out laughing. I never fully understood what the holy laughter of Abraham was until then. It seemed to make unbelief so absurd. It was as though some little fish, being very thirsty, was troubled about drinking the river dry.

God Is the God of All Comfort

Once when I was in my latter teens I was in love with a girl. It might have been puppy love, but it was real to the "puppy." We became tentatively engaged to be married, even though we were both much too young. However, she was torn in her heart and felt that the Lord was leading her to another young man who was one of my best friends, and who was already an experienced young clergyman. I suffered a broken heart and I remember going to a clergyman friend of mine to seek his help. He turned me to 2 Corinthians 1:3,4,6:

> Praise be to the God and Father of our Lord Jesus Christ, the Father of compassion and the God of all comfort, who comforts us in all our troubles, so that we can comfort those in any trouble with the comfort we ourselves have received from God. . . . if we are comforted, it is for your comfort, which produces in you patient endurance of the same sufferings we suffer.

From those words of the apostle I gained comfort for myself in my personal trouble, just as many others have also done. But there is more to it than that. This passage from Paul suggests a new insight into suffering. Briefly put, it is this: not only are we comforted in our trials, but *our trials can equip us to comfort others.*

It is an undeniable fact that usually it is those who have suffered most who are best able to comfort others who are passing through suffering. I know of pastors whose ministries have been enriched by suffering. Through their trials they have learned to "live through" the difficulties of the people in their parish. They are able to empathize as well as sympathize with the afflictions of others because of what they have experienced in their own lives.

Our sufferings may be rough and hard to bear, but they teach us lessons which in turn equip and enable us to help others. Our attitude toward suffering should not be, "Grit your teeth and bear it," hoping it will pass as quickly as possible. Rather, our goal should be to learn all we can from what we are called upon to endure, so that we can fulfill a ministry of comfort—as Jesus did. "Because he himself suffered when he was tempted, he is able to help those who are being tempted" (Heb. 2:18). The sufferer becomes the comforter or helper in the service of the Lord.

*In a crisis it is impossible to get
spiritual energy from others. Store
it up ahead of time.*
GEORGE WILLIAMS

13/

How to Prepare for Suffering

WHAT WOULD YOU do if the major cities in your country were suddenly leveled by guided missiles or enemy bombers? How would you react to the seizure of all major industries, utilities, and schools? Or what if you were taken hostage by a group of terrorists? If you have never experienced the impact of such horrors, you probably have no answer to these questions.

In the event of a national catastrophe, what does the Christian do? What should his attitude be? Which way would he turn? What if persecution should come to the church in America as it has come in many other countries?

As a whole, America (in comparison with many other areas of the world) does not know what privation is. We have little conception as a nation of what real sacrifice and suffering mean.

The immunity from persecution which Christians in some countries of the world have experienced in the past two or three centuries is unusual. We have been living through an abnormal period, especially in recent years. Christianity has been almost popular, and in America it certainly is at the time I write. Look at the hundreds of Christian books which are published every year. There are Christian movies as well as

Christian television and radio programs. One of the oldest and most prestigious American magazines has recently assumed a Christian tone. However, in my judgment, the time of this popularity will be shortened as secular materialism eats away at the vitals of the country.

In other parts of the world to be a Christian automatically exposes one to hardship, if not real persecution. Christ strongly warned His followers that to believe in Him would not be popular and that they should be prepared to face suffering and affliction for His sake.

Suffering Isn't Subnormal

The Bible says that all who want "to live a godly life in Christ Jesus will be persecuted" (2 Tim. 3:12). Jesus said that as the time of His return draws nigh, "they will lay hands on you and persecute you" (Luke 21:12).

We have no scriptural foundation for believing that we can forever escape being physically persecuted for Christ's sake. The fact that we are *not* being persecuted is an abnormal condition. The normal condition for Christians is that they should suffer persecution.

Since we have experienced little religious persecution in this country, it is likely that under pressure many would deny Christ. It is entirely conceivable that the persecution of Christian believers now taking place in other parts of the world may also come to such areas as Europe, Australia, Canada, and America.

Dr. Donald Coggan, the former Archbishop of Canterbury, in an address in London referred to his recent visit to a certain country and told of how he had seen something firsthand of the witness of Christians under persecution.

He said, "the faith of Christians is being tested in the fire. What a witness is theirs! How should we fare, I wonder, in similar circumstances? Are we too soft, cushy, easy in Britain to be able to stand up to persecution? Should we defect? Or should we, like so many of them, triumph?"

This is a question to be seriously pondered. If persecution came, what would you and I do? For the most part we would do no more, no less, than we are doing right now. Some of us who shout the loudest about our faith would surrender soonest. Many who boast of being courageous would be the most cowardly. Many like Peter who say, "Though all others deny Christ, yet I will never deny him," would be the first to warm their hands at the campfires of the enemy.

In speaking of the last times, Jesus warned, "Then you will be handed over to be persecuted and put to death, and you will be hated by all nations because of me" (Matt. 24:9). He also said, "Because of the increase of wickedness, the love of most will grow cold" (Matt. 24:12). Paul, referring to the conflict with "the spiritual forces of evil" wrote, "Therefore put on the full armor of God, so that when the day of evil comes, you may be able to stand your ground, and after you have done everything, to stand" (Eph. 6:13).

Here are five points to use as a checklist in determining the full strength of your "full armor." Write them down, refer to them daily, and act upon them.

Look Godward

First, we must make sure of our relationship to God. As Amos the prophet saw the day of judgment fast approaching for Israel, he warned the people to prepare to meet God (Amos 4:12). The word *preparedness* should be a key word for everyone.

It is strange that we prepare for everything except meeting God. We prepare for marriage and for a career. We prepare for athletic contests. A person attempting to be on an Olympic team anywhere in the world practices his or her sport several hours a day, perhaps for years, before he considers himself prepared. But we do not prepare to meet God. Even though most of us see the storm clouds gathering on the horizon, by and large we are making few preparations to meet God. This is a time for repentance and faith. It is a time for soul-searching, a time to see if our anchor holds.

Walk with God

Second, we should learn now to walk with God in our daily life.

Abraham walked with God and was called a friend of God (Isa. 41:8; James 2:23). Walk with God as Noah did; when the flood came, Noah was saved. Walk with God as Moses did in the solitude of the desert; when the hour of judgment fell upon Egypt, Moses was prepared to lead his people to victory. Walk with God as David did as a shepherd boy; when he was called to rule his people he was prepared for the task of kingship. Daniel and his three young friends walked with God in Babylon, and when trouble came, God was beside them— whether it was in the lions' den or in the fiery furnace.

However, the Bible teaches that God does not always deliver His saints from adversity. As we have seen, a careful reading of Hebrews 11 shows that *"others"* were just as faithful as Abraham, Moses, Daniel, or David; they, too, walked with God—but they perished. God has not promised to deliver us *from* trouble, but He has promised to go *with us through* the trouble.

Stephen was a young man "full of faith and of the Holy Spirit" (Acts 6:5). They stoned him to death, but *his* was a triumphal entry into heaven. If you are not strengthening the inner man now by daily walking with God, when a crisis comes you will quake with fear and give in, having no strength to stand up for Christ.

Work with the Word

Third, we need to fortify ourselves with the Word of God. Begin reading, studying, and memorizing Scripture as never before.

Paul says, "Stand firm then, with the belt of truth buckled around your waist" (Eph. 6:14). The truth is the Word of God. He also says, "Take the . . . sword of the Spirit, which is the word of God" (v.17). We are to be girded and undergirded with the Word. To achieve this, we must read it, assimilate it, feed on it. We must let it be our staff and strength. It is quick and powerful—the bulwark of the soul.

To many, Scripture is little more than a reference book of biblical facts. It is seldom opened and rarely relished as the spiritual staff of life which it is. Many Christians are anemic and starved for the things of God. They are totally unprepared for a time of crisis or conflict. We need to make the Scriptures a daily part of our lives, storing God's Word in our hearts and minds. Then, if our Bible is ever taken away from us we can readily recall it, feed upon it, and inwardly digest it.

Countless stories have come out of prison camps of Christians who had no Bibles but who had committed to memory great portions of Scripture. What a comfort, blessing and strength those Scriptures were as they repeated them over and over again to themselves. One Christian who was in a prison camp for three years told me that during his imprisonment his greatest regret was not having memorized more of the Bible.

Practice Prayer

Fourth, we need to fortify ourselves with prayer. The Bible, referring to "the evil day," says, "Pray in the Spirit on all occasions with all kinds of prayers and requests" (Eph. 6:18). If we are to stand uncompromisingly for Christ when a national crisis comes, we must rediscover the power of prayer. Jesus taught us that we should "always pray and not give up" (Luke 18:1).

The early church knew the value and necessity of prayer. Earnest, fervent prayer preceded every major triumph. Prayer preceded Pentecost.

The church in Jerusalem prayed in time of persecution, and as a result "they were all filled with the Holy Spirit and spoke the word of God boldly" (Acts 4:31). When the apostle Peter was imprisoned by King Herod, the believers in Jerusalem prayed and he was miraculously released (Acts 12:1–17).

Paul and Silas prayed in prison; the Philippian jailer found Christ, and the prisoners were delivered (Acts 16:25–34).

If Christianity is to survive in a godless and materialistic world, we must repent of our prayerlessness. We must make prayer our priority. The prayer meeting should be the most important and meaningful service of any church.

In the Old Testament we read of a wicked, pagan, powerful king by the name of Sennacherib. This Assyrian leader had made his boastful announcement that he would by force subdue God's people and possess their land. His propaganda machine went into action. He sent messages to Israel saying,

"Who of all the gods of these nations that my fathers destroyed has been able to save his people from me? How then can your god deliver you from my hand?" (2 Chron. 32:14).

Assyria had built a vast and formidable war machine which had run ruthlessly over the nations of Judah and Israel. In the arms race of their day the Assyrians were definitely ahead! Their armored soldiers policed the subdued, conquered countries just as is happening in some countries today. The whole world trembled when Sennacherib spoke!

Hezekiah, Israel's king, realized that on the purely human level the Assyrians could make good their proud boasts. They were superior in manpower and arms; no nation had been able to withstand them. Hezekiah knew full well that without God's help his people would be wiped off the face of the earth. He trusted in God implicitly—and *his secret weapon was prayer.*

The Bible says, "King Hezekiah and the prophet Isaiah son of Amoz cried out in prayer to heaven about this" (2 Chron. 32:20). Get this dramatic picture: a king and a prophet of God on their knees before God in earnest prayer. Then a miracle happened!

The account continues: "And the Lord sent an angel, who annihilated all the fighting men and the leaders and officers in the camp of the Assyrian king. So he [Sennacherib] withdrew to his own land in disgrace. . . . So the Lord saved Hezekiah and the people of Jerusalem from the hand of Sennacherib king of Assyria and from the hand of all others. He took care of them on every side" (2 Chron. 32:21,22). Miracles have happened in history when God's people have turned to Him in prayer. His word to us is still this: "Call upon me in the day of trouble; I will deliver you, and you will honor me" (Ps. 50:15).

A call for national and individual repentance is urgently needed today, or judgment is certain to fall. I believe in being prepared as a nation, in being so strong that we will not invite attack. But no amount of military preparation can take the place of spiritual preparedness. We need the inner strength that comes from a personal, vital relationship with God through His Son Jesus Christ.

I read an article recently in a British newspaper whose

headline asked: "Britain—Will it Survive?" The writer went on to say that five years from now, unless Britain has a moral and spiritual reawakening, it will be in the grip of a new type of atheistic, materialistic government.

The first thing Hezekiah and Isaiah did when a national crisis broke over their land was to fall upon their knees before Almighty God. They did not pray for God to be on their side, but they prayed that they might be on God's side. In answer to their earnest pleas and because of their consistently righteous way of life, God sent a battalion of heavenly warriors to deliver them.

But God does not always deliver His children out of crises and catastrophe. For example, during the trials and tribulations of the '70s, many people in Uganda prayed earnestly to the Lord to deliver them. The evil regime in that country has taken the lives of many believers. The Lord delivered them, but not in the way they had expected. It is up to us as Christians to accept whatever God sends, and to be prepared in our hearts and minds for change and revolution—and even torture and death.

Corrie ten Boom tells how, in the midst of the horrors of Ravensbruck prison camp, she learned to pray. Prayer was her constant resort. Through prayer she knew the reality of Christ in her life, even when the burdens were quite overwhelming. She prayed, "Lord, teach me to cast all my burdens upon Thee and go on without them. Only Thy Spirit can teach me that lesson. Give me Thy Spirit, O Lord, and I shall have faith, such faith that I shall no longer carry a load of care."

Practice the Presence of Christ

Fifth, we must fortify ourselves by realizing the nearness of the Lord at all times. Spurgeon once said, "There have never been fifteen minutes in my life when I did not sense the presence of Christ." I regret I cannot say that. We must learn again to practice the presence of Christ, not only in days of testing and suffering, but always.

We are surely encouraged to do that by Christ's final promise to His disciples after He had commissioned them to go and make disciples of all nations. He said, "I will be with you always, to the very end of the age" (Matt. 28:20). It is a promise for obedient disciples, and it is marvellously inclusive.

Dr. Handley Moule, sometime Anglican Bishop of Durham, England and a noted Greek scholar, maintained that the *always* could be paraphrased to mean, "I am with you all the days, all day long." That means we can count on Christ's presence not only every day, but every moment of every day. Of the *fact* of His presence there can be no doubt, for His Word cannot fail. What we need is to cultivate the *sense* of His presence, every day, every hour, every moment.

A few years ago my wife Ruth had a terrible fall. She suffered a concussion, was unconscious for nearly a week, broke her foot in five places, and injured her hip. When she regained consciousness she found she had lost a great deal of her memory. What disturbed her most was that she had forgotten so many of the Scriptures she had learned throughout the years. The verses of a whole lifetime were more precious to her than all earthly possessions.

One night when she was praying, because she was so distressed, out of nowhere came the verse, "I have loved thee with an everlasting love. . . ." She has no recollection of ever memorizing this verse, but the Lord brought it back to her. Gradually, other verses began to come back. But interestingly, while she was still trying to recover her memory, she memorized Romans 8:31-39 and repeated these verses over and over again:

What, then, shall we say in response to this? If God is for us, who can be against us? He who did not spare his own Son, but gave him up for us all—how will he not also, along with him, graciously give us all things? Who will bring any charge against those whom God has chosen? It is God who justifies. Who is he that condemns? Christ Jesus, who died—more than that, who was raised to life—is at the right hand of God and is also interceding for us. Who shall separate us from the love of Christ? Shall trouble or hardship or persecution or famine or nakedness or danger or sword? As it is written: "For your sake we face death all day long; we are considered as sheep to be slaughtered." No, in all these things we are more than conquerors through him who loved us. For I am convinced that neither death nor life, neither angels nor demons, neither the present nor the future, nor any powers, neither height nor depth, nor anything else in all creation, will be able to separate us from the love of God that is in Christ Jesus our Lord.

I urge you to memorize this passage. Hide it away in your heart. When persecution, trouble, and adversity arise, these verses will come back to you a thousand times.

Christ must be vitally real to us if we are to remain faithful to Him in the hour of crisis. And who knows how near that hour may be? The wheels of God's judgment can be heard by discerning people in the assembly of the United Nations, in the conferences of political leaders, in the offices of the editors of great newspapers or television networks around the world—and among the people throughout the nations. Things are happening fast! The need for a turning to God has never been more urgent.

The words of Isaiah, whom God used to confound an ancient, godless aggressor, are appropriate for us today: "Seek the Lord while he may be found; call on him while he is near. Let the wicked forsake his way and the evil man his thoughts. Let him turn to the Lord, and he will have mercy on him, and to our God, for he will freely pardon" (55:6,7).

David proved that outward armor is not nearly so important as the man within the armor. Unless men of purpose, integrity, and faith stand together in unswerving loyalty to Jesus Christ, the future of the world is dark indeed.

Strengthen the Family

To prepare ourselves for the suffering and persecution which seems so inevitable, we need also to foster and strengthen the small group movement, the concept of "Christian cells." One obvious area where this process should take place is in the family. In the United States today, as well as in other parts of the world, we are witnessing the breakdown and erosion of the family unit. Divorce is rampant and "living together" without the formality of a wedding ceremony is increasingly common. It is only the strong Christian family unit that can survive the coming world holocaust.

To prepare for the crisis to come, we need to nurture and

undergird the family unit. The previous points I have mentioned can be applied to our family lives. *First*, we need to place God at the center of our family life and make Him the circumference as well. *Second*, as a family we need to walk with God daily. *Third*, consulting and memorizing Scripture *as a family* is vital. Not a day should go by without a time of family fellowship around the Word of God. Together the family should "read, mark, learn and inwardly digest" the Scriptures as an essential preparation for the persecution ahead.

Family prayer is the *fourth* vital link in the chain of spiritual strength—a strength we are trying to build to protect us from a world gone mad. The habit of praying together as a family is one of the most strengthening factors in unifying and energizing the members of that family to go out into a troubled world. Only by direct contact with God through prayer can we hope to have the serenity and security that will enable us to witness for Christ in the world outside. The practice of prayer as a family also equips its individual members to pray effectively amid the pressures of daily living. The home is the best place to learn spiritual lessons such as these.

What I have said about the family unit is also true concerning the value of the small, intimate groups or fellowships springing up inside and outside the organized church today. When brothers and sisters in Christ unite in the common bond of the Word of God and prayer, they are strengthened in their faith and witness. The support of others is especially helpful when suffering comes. Scripture urges us to bear "one another's burdens, and so fulfill the law of Christ" (Gal. 6:2, KJV); to "encourage one another and build each other up" (1 Thess. 5:11). This can best be done in small Christian groups; and when it is done, amazing things can happen.

For example, we are learning that the church in China has survived the more than twenty-five years of severe restrictions. How? Through the health and existence of "house churches." These consist of small groups of believers, who, though driven "underground" during the cultural revolution, managed to meet regularly around the Word. Despite the concerted effort to destroy all the Bibles in China, some copies survived and around these, or the verses and even passages believers had memorized, small groups of Christians met. Chinese Christians in prisons and labor camps have allowed the flame of their faith to burn brightly and have been used to lead other Chinese to the Lord.

What about ourselves? The challenge is a personal one and concerns each one of us. In the end, the best way we can prepare for suffering of any kind is by seeking continually to deepen our spiritual lives—by which I mean *to deepen our life in the Spirit.*

The apostle Paul's exhortation to the Christians of his day was to "be filled with the Spirit" (Eph. 5:18). It was not merely a counsel: it was a command. And the verb in the Greek is in the present tense, conveying the idea of continuance. "Keep on being filled with the Spirit" is what Paul is saying here. This is not a one-time happening, but an ongoing experience. We are to be catch basins for the fullness of God. Like a freshly running spring, we are to overflow and let our lives touch the lives of those around us.

This is the way we are to prepare for whatever is in store for us in the critical and testing times that lie ahead. When the "evil day" comes, we shall have to be dependent not on the circumstances around us, but on the hidden resources within us. And those resources are not of ourselves but of God. Be filled with the Spirit!

*It is by those who have suffered
that the world has been advanced.*
LEO TOLSTOY

14/

*How to Help Those
Who Are Hurt*

FOR THE MOST part this book has been concerned with suffering in the more generally accepted sense—the sort of suffering associated with physical pain and illness, and with open hostility and persecution.

But there are other aspects of suffering which cannot be ignored or overlooked in a book of this kind. This is the suffering caused by the "hurts" of life which we all too easily inflict on others, or of which we ourselves are sometimes the victims.

Some might be inclined to dismiss such injuries as comparatively unimportant. But they are real enough and by no means trivial. They concern us all in our everyday lives. They concern you who read this chapter.

Your life is intricately woven into the lives of scores and hundreds of others around you. Consider the variety of lives that you influence in one day: your family members and their friends, business associates, neighbors, grocery store attendants, service station attendants, waitresses, bus drivers, your pastor, fellow church members. Whether these relationships are casual or deeply rooted, the potential exists within each one for great hurt or great help.

Somewhere within your circle of contacts someone is being hurt. Are you aware of it? What can you do to help that person? Are you the source of that person's hurt? Or are you the one who is hurt? How should you react?

In this chapter we want to explore these questions. God wants us to become increasingly sensitive to the feelings and needs of those around us. And He wants us to learn how to deal properly with our own hurts.

How We Hurt Others

Sometimes we hurt others deliberately and sometimes inadvertently.

In her recently published book, *Please Don't Shoot!: I'm Already Wounded,* "Hansi" (Maria Ann Hirschmann) tells us what happened when her husband left her. She admits to having been an overly strict, hard mother who had driven her children from her. In the devastation she experienced aftei having been deserted by both husband and children, she was further hurt by the criticism and the attitude of former Christian friends. After being tenderly and lovingly dealt with by the Lord, she honestly faced up to her own shortcomings and allowed the Lord to change her. In speaking to a group of women one day she felt led to share her experience and was floored by the response. Scores of women, she has found over the years, have been just as deeply hurt and have found Christians to be not only unsympathetic but disapproving, condemning, and downright cruel. In time, as Hansi allowed the Lord to deal with her and change her, she was reconciled to each of her children and finally reached the point where she was able to pray for her former husband and his new wife. I hope her book will help Christians realize that being judgmental and condemning is not one of the gifts of the Spirit.

Then there is the story of Somerset Maugham's mother. It is said that she was an extraordinarily beautiful woman, married to an extraordinarily ugly man. Later on in life a close friend teasingly asked her how she had managed, being such a beautiful woman herself, to stay married to such an ugly man. She thought a moment and replied quite seriously, "He never once hurt my feelings."

As these stories show, we hurt others when we are unkind. Few Christians are deliberately unkind. Perhaps it is just that they do not realize the effect their course of action, their tone of voice, or what they say is having on a certain individual. One of our children had the experience of having a kind teacher one year and an unkind one the next year. This repeated itself for several years. It was interesting to see the way she flourished under the kind teachers and regressed under the unkind ones.

I think this was also true in my own life. Often the only thing a child can remember about an adult in later years, when he or she is grown, is whether or not that person was kind.

"The nicest thing that we can do for our heavenly Father," someone has said, "is to be kind to one of His children." That is true, I know, because of how deeply grateful I am when someone is kind to one of mine.

Gossip is another way in which we hurt others. "May the absent always feel safe with us" is a motto to be remembered.

There are parents who have done what they could to bring up their children "in the nurture and admonition of the Lord," only to have them reject not only what they had been taught but their parents themselves.

Do you have a friend with such a child? If so, what have you done? Have you been judgmental, critical, gossiping, and perhaps smug because your children are staunch believers wholly committed to the Lord?

This little poem speaks vividly to us on the subject:

> They felt good eyes upon them
> and shrank within—undone;
> good parents had good children
> and they—a wandering one.
>
> The good folks never meant
> to act smug or condemn,
> but having prodigals
> just "wasn't done" with them.
>
> Remind them gently, Lord,
> how You
> have trouble with Your children,
> too.[1]

---

1. Ruth Bell Graham, *Sitting by My Laughing Fire* (Waco: Word Books, 1977), p. 47.

We must always remember how God hates sin, yet is so tender and compassionate with the sinner. How often we fail to make the distinction.

Then there is criticizing. Criticism usually discourages. Have you noticed how, when you read your Bible, you find God telling you all of your mistakes, sins, and shortcomings without once discouraging you? That is because at the same time His love comes shining through and with it the promise of His presence and power to help us overcome. Criticism from people usually has a withering effect. This is especially true, I think, when dealing with our children. They need guidance and correcting; but if only somehow we could learn to be more encouraging! If they are messy in their rooms, encourage them when they straighten things up. If they are habitually late, praise them when they make it on time. In Psalm 72 is David's prayer for his son, Solomon. Verse 15 says, "Prayer also shall be made for him continually; *and* daily shall he be praised" (KJV). What a suggestion for parents! Pray continually—praise daily. Failure to do this will cause more damage than we may be able to repair.

Failing to encourage is one of the commonest ways to hurt other people. "More people fail through discouragement," someone has said, "than for any other reason."

Another way we hurt people is by being too busy. Too busy to notice their needs. Too busy to drop that note of comfort or encouragement or assurance of love. Too busy to listen when someone needs to talk. Too busy to care. When Alan Redpath was pastor at The Moody Church, Chicago, he had hanging on the wall of his study these words: "Beware of the barrenness of a busy life."

The wife who fails to be supportive of her husband can hurt him as an individual and also hurt his work. This is also true of the husband who fails to be supportive of his wife. Even such an apparently insignificant thing as the tone of voice can have a devastating effect. It has been pointed out that more friction and tensions are caused in a family by tone of voice than for any other one reason.

The psychologists tell us of the need for people to have both security and significance. While only God can provide ultimate security and enable a person to realize his or her true significance, we as parents who fail to make our children feel secure in our love, and help them to realize their own individual significance and worth, leave them scarred for life.

Then there is the one in authority who over-represses. This may be a husband who does not allow his wife to express herself or to disagree with him. Every man needs to be disagreed with occasionally. I know of one such man who, incredible as it may seem, made it clear to his wife when they were first married that she was never to disagree with him. At one point later on in life when they had a well-known Christian leader as a guest for dinner, the guest took exception to something said by the host and was ordered out of the home by the wife saying, "No one disagrees with my husband under my roof!" This may sound like fiction, but it is true. That man, though extremely capable and talented, grew to be uncomfortably arrogant. In Ecclesiastes 8:9 we have this interesting comment, "There is a time when a man lords it over others to his own hurt."

We never gain in life by hurting others. Sometimes we try to elevate our own insecure egos by degrading and belittling those around us. Yet this produces only a false sense of self-esteem.

On the contrary, Scripture teaches us to be more concerned about the needs and feelings of others than our own. We are to encourage and build self-confidence in our loved ones, friends, and associates. We are to encourage their growth as individuals and applaud their successes. Someone has said that a true servant of God is someone who helps another succeed.

Often we will experience greater satisfaction and joy over the accomplishments of others than our own. A good definition of "joy" worth remembering is formed by the following acrostic:

> *J*esus first.
> *O*thers second.
> *Y*ourself last.

How We React to Being Hurt

I know of a man who was tortured unbelievably for his faith in Christ. He made it a point when undergoing torture, to pray for the individual (or individuals) torturing him. On regaining his freedom, he returned to civilization a warm, normal, compassionate man. I read about another who suffered in similar circumstances, but who came out a spiritually wounded man—resentful and bitter.

The way in which we react to hurts and disappointments influences the shaping of our personalities, and it can also deeply affect our families and friends.

Sometimes we become resentful, defensive, or vindictive.

It is a fact, strange as it might seem, that abused children frequently grow up to be abusive parents. One would think it would have the opposite effect—that a child who had known hurt and suffering would determine to be the sort of parent he himself had never had.

Years ago we were given a Saint Bernard puppy in Switzerland. The first week we had her, she fell off the second-story porch and broke her leg. I still carry the scar on my finger where she bit me when I went to help her. Many a hurt person bites the hand reaching out to help.

We can react to hurt negatively or positively, self-centeredly or God-centeredly. The latter will produce a clear perspective on our situation and will promote the building of a healthier personality.

Let me share with you a few ideas on how God wants us to react to hurt.

By Trusting in God's Sovereignty

A prisoner recently released from years at hard labor, without a Bible, drew for his spiritual nourishment on the passages of Scripture which he had memorized since his conversion as a young boy. One he mentioned particularly was Psalm 66. As I read that Psalm I was impressed by the fact that the psalmist recognized no secondary causes. Beginning with verse 10 he says, "For *you,* O God, tested us; *you* refined us like silver." Verse 11, *"You* brought us into prison and laid burdens on our backs." Verse 12, *"You* let men ride over our heads; we went through fire and water, but *you* brought us to a place of abundance" (italics mine).

In the Scriptures we find this also true in the case of Job. Job did not know that Satan had to get permission from God before he could touch Job, much less Job's possessions. Yet when Job had lost everything he did not say, "The Lord gave and the devil has taken away," but "The Lord gave and the Lord has taken away; may the name of the Lord be praised" (Job 1:21).

So when we are hurt it is important to remember that God Himself has allowed it for a purpose.

By Forgiving Those Who Hurt Us

When we are hurt by the careless or deliberate actions and words of another, God calls us to extend forgiveness. This will help heal the relationship we have with the person, and it will keep us from being poisoned by our own bitterness. "Be kind and compassionate to one another, forgiving each other, just as in Christ God forgave you" (Eph. 4:32).

By Being Patient

Writing to Christians who were suffering for their faith, James said:

Be *patient*, then, brothers, until the Lord's coming. See how the farmer waits for the land to yield its valuable crop and how patient he is for the fall and spring rains. You too, be patient and stand firm, because the Lord's coming is near (James 5:7,8, italics mine).

Patience is not simply a "teeth-clenched," complacent endurance of a particular situation. It is an attitude of expectation. The farmer was able to stare at his seemingly barren ground with patience because he was assured that there would be results of his labors. He could have patience in his labors because there would be products of his labors.

And so it is in the spiritual realm. As we have seen, God can produce valuable qualities in our lives through the hurts and sufferings we experience. We can suffer patiently, for our suffering will yield a spiritual harvest.

And we can suffer during this life patiently, for we know that in God's perfect time His Son will return as the greatest reward for the waiting and working believer.

By Giving Thanks

In 1 Thessalonians 5:18, the Christian is instructed to "give thanks in *all* circumstances, for this is God's will for you in Christ Jesus" (italics mine). A faculty member wrote in the "Montreat-Anderson College Newsletter" recently (Spring, 1980):

> In the midst of life situations, one is to offer thanksgiving. Thanksgiving is not molded by one's circumstances, but it is based upon the integrity of God's character and the infallibility of His purposes.
> What does thanksgiving do for the believer? It gives him:
> —A New Focus . . .
> . . . from self to God.
> —A New Perspective . . .
> . . . from one's problems and perplexities
> to God's purpose and priorities.
> —A New Attitude . . .
> . . . from anxiety to assurance. Calm is the
> heart that rests upon the certainty of
> God's control.
> —A New Enterprise . . .
> . . . God can use the believer in any given
> situation to further His purposes and bring glory to His name.
> Furthermore, thanksgiving promotes a healthy Body. It encourages and edifies fellow believers. Thanksgiving is an exercise worth cultivating and serves as an antidote to complacency. What's more, it's contagious!
> "Through Him then, let us continually offer up a sacrifice of praise to God, that is, the fruit of lips that give thanks to His name." (Heb. 13:15)

God wants His children to be happy and healthy. And He can show each of us how to react to hurts so that they will become stepping-stones to a more productive and satisfying life.

How to Help Those Who Are Suffering

Because God has given us the mandate to "love our neighbors as ourselves," and because we have witnessed this principle supremely demonstrated in the life and death of His Son, we must take seriously our call to minister to our neighbor who suffers.

The first thing we should do is ask the Lord to give us love, sensitivity to the situation, and His wisdom.

It is of utmost importance that we be sensitive to each individual, to each situation, in order to determine the immediate priorities.

Our son, Franklin, spent some days on a boat in the South China Seas searching for boat people fleeing the oppressive regime in Vietnam. On board, Ha Jimmy, the first mate, told him how the week before they had rescued such a boat. It had been boarded by pirates, the passengers robbed, women raped, others wounded. The pirate ship was ramming the smaller boat to destroy all evidence when the rescue ship appeared and they fled.

First, the wounded had to be tended to. Then the rescued needed to be fed, bathed, and allowed to rest. Later they were told of Jesus and His love.

One mother on board with several small children saw her baby die. There was nothing to do but put the tiny body overboard and watch it float away. A few days later the next child died. Once more the mother had to watch the little body floating away into the sea.

Ha Jimmy looked at Franklin, his eyes dark with fatigue, and asked, "Franklin, after all she had been through, if I hadn't given her Jesus, what had I really done for her?"

God can use a sensitive Christian to be a rich blessing in the life of one who knows pain and sorrow. Scripture provides guidelines for those who are in a position to help someone suffering.

1. "Weep with those who weep." If not actual tears, it means we suffer with them.

Job's friends were correct to come to the poor man's home and sit with him. They were of comfort to Job until they opened their mouths. Sometimes the greatest sermon is silence! A suffering person does not need a lecture—he needs a listener. He needs someone to whom he can pour out his heart or someone who will share his silence. Most of all, he needs someone who will share his grief.

Jesus was acutely sensitive to those in suffering situations. Upon seeing the widow of Nain accompanying the funeral bier of her son, we are told Jesus "had compassion." The meaning in the Greek is that "His heart went out to her." Jesus had great compassion in the face of death. On this particular occasion, He did not deliver a sermon. He met the woman's deepest need, the need to know that God was aware of her situation and that He cared. Jesus gave a powerful demonstration of this by raising the boy from the dead.

When Jesus' good friend Lazarus died, Jesus came to the home and wept. He knew that He was victor over death. He knew that soon He would perform the miracle of raising Lazarus from the dead and thereby prove He could conquer man's greatest fear—the dread of the tomb.

Yet, *He wept.* Lazarus' sisters were grief stricken—and Jesus joined them in their grief.

Death is difficult to face. Sometimes we are not so much shocked by someone's passing, as we are gripped by death's finality. Although we may trust God's promises for life after death and the certainty of a heavenly home, we must still face the reality of death.

Jesus wept with those in grief—and we must do the same.

2. "Bear one another's burdens."

Besides sharing our hearts and our ears with someone suffering, as we are able we must be ready and willing to share our material possessions and our time. We have a fine example of this in the parable of the Good Samaritan.

Upon finding a man robbed, beaten, and left for dead, the Samaritan did not continue on to his destination and "report the accident." Nor did he pay someone else to go back and care for the man. The Samaritan himself got involved.

He tenderly lifted the wounded body onto his own donkey and cautiously continued on the journey to Jericho. Upon reaching the city, he secured lodging. During the night he probably cared for the patient, tenderly nursing his wounds. The next day, he made arrangements with the innkeeper to pay all financial debts that the patient would incur.

This is how God wants us to treat the suffering.

In Galatians 6:2, we are instructed to "bear . . . one another's burdens, and so fulfil the law of Christ" (KJV). Everyone is designed to be able to assume his own individual level of responsibilities and pressures. But when his load goes beyond the breaking point, another is to come along and help—and sometimes that help can be given through material possessions.

May God give us the sensitivity to recognize these needs in those around us.

3. Pray for those who are hurt, and where possible or advisable also pray with them and share Scripture.

It can be a great comfort when someone shares with us in prayer and leads us to "the throne of grace" where we can "find grace to help us in our time of need" (Heb. 4:16).

Rather than Christian friends giving us personal advice in the midst of the crisis, how much better for them to share God's loving promises with us. It is a comfort to hear the words of God in times of stress. The Holy Spirit can take God's word of truth and minister it to our deepest needs.

Be careful before leaving someone in a sorrowing situation. Say a word of prayer with them and share even a brief word of encouragement from the Scriptures.

These are just a few suggestions for helping those who suffer. Let us remember three things in conclusion:

1. Those who have suffered make the best comforters. When we are in trouble we turn for help to those who have suffered and who we know will understand: our Lord Himself, the psalmist, Paul "the prisoner of Jesus Christ," and down through the centuries those who have suffered and who, from their sufferings, have ministered to a suffering world—not always writers, but painters, musicians, sculptors, and so on. The list grows and ends in the memory of God. For only God knows all who in a multitude of small, quickly forgotten ways have eased the load of another.

When my father-in-law died, those who were the greatest comfort to his widow were not necessarily the Scripture quoters, but other widows, her friends, who never said a word: they just held her in their arms as they wept together.

2. Our help must extend beyond our own social register. I think a good example here would be of the Good Samaritan,

who, being a Samaritan, was hated and despised by the Jews, and yet when he found a Jewish man in trouble went out of his way to show him kindness.

3. We express ourselves to the world through our physical bodies. We are the body of Christ. He expresses Himself to the world through us. As He came not to be ministered to, but to minister, so too, we must go out seeking those we can help in the name of Jesus—not necessarily in some big way, but in whatever way we can.

*What man can live and not see death,
or save himself from the power of the
grave?*

PSALM 89:48

15/

Death and How to Face It

WHEN SIR WILLIAM Russell, the English patriot, went to his execution in 1683, he took his watch out of his pocket and handed it to the physician who attended him in his death. "Would you kindly take my timepiece?" he asked, "I have no use for it. I am now dealing with eternity."

The Bible has much to say about the brevity of life, and the necessity of preparing for eternity. Although most of us live as if we were indestructible, we need a new awareness of the fact that death is rapidly approaching for all of us. The Bible has many warnings about how we should prepare to meet God. The rich with all their wealth cannot buy a reprieve from the death sentence that hangs over every man. The poor cannot beg one extra day of life from the "grim reaper" who pursues every man from the cradle to the grave.

The Scripture says, "What is your life? You are a mist that appears for a little while and then vanishes" (James 4:14).

Thanatology has become a popular subject at many colleges and universities in America. It is not only a study of death itself, but of how to prepare for death. Mostly the students are being told how to prepare for death without any reference to God. In recent years, books by Dr. Elisabeth Kübler-Ross,

Dr. Raymond A. Moody, and Dr. Maurice Rawlings have been highly publicized. Because of the terrorism throughout the world, and the many deaths caused by terrible diseases such as cancer and heart attacks, there is a new interest in death.

If you listen to some of the popular music that young people are singing, it is difficult for the older generation to understand the words. But the youth get the message. If you buy a book and study the lyrics, as I have done, you will find that many of the songs deal with suffering and death.

Many a person who is cynical and secular has actually thought deeply about life and eternity. The person who may be the life of the party may also be the one who is wearing a mask. Underneath there is a deep dread and fear of death and eternity. In a recent survey it was found that young people think more about death than any other subject except sex. I am convinced that if people gave more thought to death, eternity, judgment, and hell, there would be more holy living and a greater consciousness of God.

Too many Christians try to put off the thought of death and of one day standing before the judgment seat of Christ to give an account of how they spent their time here on earth.

The Bible says that man's days are "swifter than a *weaver's shuttle*" (Job 7:6, italics mine). In the Carolinas and in England I have visited the textile mills and have watched the giant looms which turn out cloth for the world. The shuttles move with the speed of lightning, scarcely visible to the naked eye. The Bible says man's life here on earth is like this.

Put your hand on your heart and feel it beat. It is saying, "Quick! Quick! Quick!" Only a few brief years at the most.

It Is Like a Fleeting Shadow

Regularly we read in our newspapers about the budget of this or that nation. We now are used to the term *billions*. I wonder how many of us really ever stop to think what a billion is. Someone suggested to me, "Before you use the term again, consider what an exaggeration 'Thanks a billion' really is. Just over one billion seconds ago we were in World War II and the atomic bomb had not yet been exploded. Over one billion minutes ago Christ was still on earth. Just over one billion hours ago we were still in the caveman era."

However, in terms of government spending, one billion dollars ago is only a few hours ago because the American government's budget will be about one trillion dollars soon at the present rate of escalation.

Or have you ever stopped to compute how many days you have left? You can do it easily on your small calculator. If you live to be seventy you have approximately 25,000 days of life. If you are now thirty-five you have little more than 12,000 days left.

The Bible also teaches that life is like a *shadow,* like a fleeting cloud moving across the face of the sun. The psalmist says, "For I dwell with you as an alien, a stranger, as all my fathers were" (Ps. 39:12). The world is not a permanent home, it is only a temporary dwelling. "We are aliens and strangers in your sight, as were all our forefathers. Our days on earth are like a shadow, without hope" (1 Chron. 29:15).

For every one of us time is slipping away. The late President Kennedy never dreamed on that Friday morning in 1963 as he ate breakfast that by two o'clock in the afternoon he would be in eternity. We never know when our moment is coming. Tragedies such as his death and that of his brother, Bobby, should help us realize the uncertainty of life, the brevity of time, and our need to be ready to meet God at any moment.

The Scripture teaches that God knows the exact moment when each person is to die (Job 14:5). There are appointed bounds beyond which we cannot pass.

I am convinced that when a person is prepared to die, he is also prepared to live. Again, if we knew all that there is to know, we would choose to die at the time God has planned for us to die.

One of the primary goals in life therefore should be to prepare for death. Everything else should be secondary.

The Tiny Blades of Opportunity

The Bible reminds us further that our days are as grass (Ps. 103:15). They are filled with tiny golden minutes with eternity in them. We are exhorted to redeem the time because the days are evil (Eph. 5:16). As C. T. Studd, the famous Cambridge cricketer and missionary pioneer, wrote while still a student at Cambridge,

Only one life, 'twill soon be past;
Only what's done for Christ will last.

Life is a glorious opportunity if it is used to condition us for eternity. If we fail in this, though we succeed in everything else, our life will have been a failure. There is no escape for the man who squanders his opportunity to prepare to meet God.

Our lives are also *immortal.* God made man different from the other creatures. He made him in His own image, a living soul. When this body dies and our earthly existence is terminated, the soul or spirit lives on forever. One hundred years from this day you will be more alive than you are at this moment. The Bible teaches that life does not end at the cemetery. There is a future life with God for those who put their trust in His Son, Jesus Christ. There is also a future hell of separation from God toward which all are going who have refused, rejected, or neglected to receive His Son, Jesus Christ.

Victor Hugo once said, "I feel in myself the future life." Cyrus the Great is reported to have declared, "I cannot imagine that the soul lives only while it remains in this mortal body." Nothing but our hope in Christ will take the sting out of death and throw a rainbow of hope around the clouds of the future life. Our anchor is in Jesus Christ, who abolished death and brought life and immortality to light through the gospel.

Death for the Christian

Most of us know what it means to be stunned by the sudden passing of a dedicated friend, a godly pastor, a devout missionary, or a saintly mother. We have stood at the open grave with hot tears coursing down our cheeks and have asked in utter bewilderment, "Why, O God, why?"

The death of the righteous is no accident. Do you think that the God whose watchful vigil notes the sparrow's fall and who knows the number of hairs on our heads would turn His back on one of His children in the hour of peril? With Him there are no accidents, no tragedies, and no catastrophes as far as His children are concerned.

Paul, who lived most of his Christian life on the brink of death, expressed triumphant certainty about life. He testified, "To me, to live is Christ and to die is gain" (Phil. 1:21). His strong, unshakeable faith took trouble, persecution, pain, thwarted plans, and broken dreams in stride.

He never bristled in questioning cynicism and asked, "Why, Lord?" He knew beyond the shadow of a doubt that his life was being fashioned into the image and likeness of his Savior; and despite the discomfort, he never flinched in the process.

Paul Knew for Sure

Things didn't always work out according to his own plans and ideas, but Paul did not murmur or question. His assurance was this: "We know that in all things God works for the good of those who love him, who have been called according to his purpose" (Rom. 8:28).

When his tired, bruised body began to weaken under the load, he said in triumph, "We know that if the earthly tent we live in is destroyed, we have a building from God, an eternal house in heaven, not built by human hands" (2 Cor. 5:1).

The world called him foolish for his belief that men could become partakers of eternal life through faith. But he jutted out his chin and said exultantly, "I know whom I have believed, and am convinced that he is able to guard what I have entrusted to him for that day" (2 Tim. 1:12).

Every one of these triumphant affirmations rings with the note of hope and the assurance of life immortal. Though the Christian has no immunity from death and no claim to perpetual life on this planet, death is to him a friend rather than a foe, the beginning rather than the end, another step on the pathway to heaven rather than a leap into a dark unknown.

For many people, the corrosive acids of materialistic science have eroded away their faith in everlasting life. But let's face it—Einstein's equation $E = MC^2$ is no satisfactory substitute for Faith + Commitment = Hope.

Paul believed in Christ and committed his all to Christ. The result was that he *knew* Christ was able to keep him forever. Strong faith and living hope are the result of unconditional commitment to Jesus Christ.

Christians Have a Glorious Hope

One of the bonuses of being a Christian is the glorious hope that extends out beyond the grave into the glory of God's tomorrow.

The Bible opens with a tragedy and ends in a triumph.

In Genesis we see the devastation of sin and death, but in the Revelation we glimpse God's glorious victory over sin and death. Revelation 14:13 says, "'Blessed are the dead who die in the Lord from now on.' 'Yes,' says the Spirit, 'they will rest from their labor, for their deeds will follow them.'"

But what is the basis of the Christian's hope of eternal life? Is our hope of life after death merely wishful thinking or blind optimism? Can we have any certainty that there is life after death and that some day those who know Christ will go to be with Him throughout eternity?

Yes! There is one great fact which gives the Christian assurance in the face of death: the *resurrection of Jesus Christ.* It is the physical, bodily resurrection of Christ that gives us confidence and hope. Because Christ rose from the dead, we know beyond doubt that death is not the end, but is merely the transition to eternal life.

Never forget that the resurrection of Christ is in many ways the central event of all history. Paul said, "If Christ has not been raised, your faith is futile; you are still in your sins. . . . If only for this life we have hope in Christ, we are to be pitied more than all men. But Christ has indeed been raised from the dead" (1 Cor. 15:17–20). The resurrection of Christ makes all the difference! Because He rose from the dead, we *know* that He was in fact the Son of God who came to save us through His death on the cross, as He claimed.

Because Christ rose from the dead, we *know* that sin and

death and Satan have been decisively defeated. And because Christ rose from the dead, we *know* there is life after death, and that if we belong to Him we need not fear death or hell. Jesus said, "I am the resurrection and the life. He who believes in me will live, even though he dies; and whoever lives and believes in me will never die" (John 11:25,26). He also promised, "In my Father's house are many rooms; if it were not so, I would have told you. I am going there to prepare a place for you. And if I go and prepare a place for you, I will come back and take you to be with me that you also may be where I am" (John 14:2,3). We know these words are true, because Jesus died on the cross and rose again from the dead. What a glorious hope we have because of Jesus' resurrection!

> No eye has seen,
>   no ear has heard,
>   no mind has conceived
>   what God has prepared for those
>   who love him
>   (1 Cor. 2:9)

Our confidence in the future is based firmly on the fact of what God has done for us in Christ. No matter what our situation may be, we need never despair because Christ is alive. "Now if we died with Christ, we believe that we will also live with him. . . . For the wages of sin is death, but the gift of God is eternal life in Christ Jesus our Lord" (Rom. 6:8,23).

The Dying Words of Christians

Death for the righteous is distinctively different from what it is for the unbeliever. It is not something to be feared, nor is it to be shunned. It is the shadowed threshold to the palace of God. No wonder Paul declared, "I desire to depart and be with Christ, which is better by far" (Phil. 1:23).

I want to share some of the statements which I have read, experienced myself, and which are set forth in the Bible about the death of a believer as distinguished from the death of an unbeliever (one who refuses or neglects to believe in Jesus Christ). There is a vast difference between the death of the two. I have talked to doctors and nurses who have held the hands of dying people, and they say there is often as much difference between the death of a Christian and a non-Christian as there is between heaven and hell.

Most Christians have a triumphant spirit in the way they face death. Some of the statements made and recorded as they were dying are thrilling:

"Our God is the God from whom cometh salvation. God is the Lord by whom we escape death," *Martin Luther.*

"Live in Christ, die in Christ, and the flesh need not fear death," *John Knox.*

"The best of all is, God is with us," *John Wesley.*

"I have pain—but I have peace, I have peace," *Richard Baxter.*

Augustus Toplady, the author of "Rock of Ages," was jubilant and triumphant as he lay dying at the age of thirty-eight. "I enjoy heaven already in my soul," he declared; "my prayers are all converted into praises."

When *Joseph Everett* was dying he said, "Glory! Glory! Glory!" and he continued exclaiming glory for over twenty-five minutes.

In my own life I have been privileged to know what some of the dying saints said before they went to heaven. My grandmother sat up in her bed, smiled, and said, "I see Jesus, and He has His hand outstretched to me. And there is Ben and he has both of his eyes and both of his legs." (Ben, my grandfather, had lost a leg and an eye at Gettysburg.)

There was an old Welsh grocer who lived near us, and my father was at his side when he was dying. He said, "Frank, can you hear that music? I've never heard such music in all my life—the orchestras, the choirs, angels singing"—and then he was gone.

The Dying Words of Unbelievers

Compare these expressions of faith with the dying words of atheists, infidels, and agnostics:

"I am abandoned by God and man! I shall go to hell! O Christ, O Jesus Christ!" *Voltaire,* the infidel.

"When I lived, I provided for everything but death; now I must die, and I am unprepared to die," *Cesare Borgia.*

"What blood, what murders, what evil councils have I followed. I am lost! I see it well!" *Charles IX,* King of France.

Thomas Paine is reported to have cried: "I would give worlds, if I had them, if *The Age of Reason* had never been published. O Lord, help me! Christ, help me! Stay with me! It is hell to be left alone!"

Death to the Christian: a Coronation

Death is said in the Bible to be a *coronation* for the Christian. The picture is that of a prince who, after his struggles and conquests in an alien land, comes to his native country and court to be crowned and honored for his deed.

I have attended a coronation, and the pomp and grandeur is magnificent. It expands my imagination to limitless heights to begin to comprehend what our coronation in heaven will be like!

The Bible says that as long as we are here on earth, we are pilgrims and strangers in a foreign land. This world is not our home; our citizenship is in heaven. To him who is faithful, Christ will give a crown of life.

Paul said, "Now there is in store for me the crown of righteousness, which the Lord, the righteous Judge, will award to me on that day—and not only to me, but also to all who have longed for his appearing" (2 Tim. 4:8).

Death is the Christian's coronation, the end of conflict and the beginning of glory in heaven.

Death Is a Rest from Labor

The Bible also speaks of death, for a Christian, as a rest from labor. The Bible says, "Blessed *are* the dead which die in the Lord . . . that they may rest from their labours" (Rev. 14:13, KJV). It is as if the Lord of the harvest says to the weary laborer, "You have been faithful in your task, come and sit in the sheltered porch of my palace and rest from your labors— enter now into the joy of your Lord."

God's saints do not enjoy much rest here on earth. They are ceaselessly busy for the Lord. Some of them accomplish more in a few years than others do in a lifetime. But their labor and toil will some day come to an end. The Bible says, "There remains . . . a Sabbath-rest for the people of God" (Heb. 4:9). That rest cannot begin until the angel of death takes them by the hand and leads them into the glorious presence of their Lord.

The apostle Paul declared, "We are confident, I say, and would prefer to be away from the body and at home with the Lord" (2 Cor. 5:8).

Death a Departure

The Bible speaks of death as a *departure*. When Paul approached the valley of the shadow of death he did not shudder with fear; rather he announced with a note of triumph, "the time has come for my departure" (2 Tim. 4:6).

The word *departure* literally means to pull up anchor and to set sail. Everything which happens prior to death is a preparation for the final voyage. Death marks the beginning, not the end. It is a solemn, decisive step in our journey to God.

Many times I have said farewell to my wife as I have departed for some distant country to proclaim the gospel. Separation always brings a tinge of sadness, but we part from one another in the sure hope that we shall meet again. In the meantime the flame of love burns brightly in her heart and in mine.

So is the hope of the believing Christian as he stands at the grave of a loved one who is with the Lord. He knows that the separation is not forever. It is a glorious truth that those who are in Christ never see each other for the last time. We say good-bye to our loved ones only until the day breaks and the shadows flee away. It is not really "good-bye" but (as the French say) "*au revoir*"—till we meet again.

Death a Transition

In addition, the Bible speaks of the death of a Christian as a *transition*. Paul wrote, "Now we know that if the earthly tent we live in is destroyed, we have a building from God, an eternal house in heaven, not built by human hands" (2 Cor. 5:1). The word *tabernacle* in the KJV means "tent" or "temporary abode."

To the Christian death is the exchanging of a tent for a building. Here we are as pilgrims or sojourners, living in a frail, flimsy home, subject to disease, pain, and peril. But at death we exchange this crumbling, disintegrating tent or body for a house not made with hands, eternal in the heavens. The wandering wayfarer comes into his own at death and is given the title to a home which will never deteriorate, for it is eternal.

Death an Exodus

Death is also said in the Bible to be an *exodus* for the Christian. We speak of being deceased as though it were the end of everything, but the word *decease* literally means "exodus" or "going out." The imagery is that of the children of Israel leaving Egypt and their former life of bondage, slavery and hardship for the Promised Land.

So death to the Christian is an exodus from the limitations, the burdens, and the bondage of this life. Victor Hugo once said, "When I go down to the grave, I can say like so many others that I have finished my day's work; but I cannot say that I have finished my life. Another day's work will begin the next morning. The tomb is not a blind alley—it is a thoroughfare. It closes with the twilight to open with the dawn."

Death therefore is not only a going out. It is also a going in. As the Easter hymn puts it, "Jesus lives! henceforth is death but the gate of life immortal."

A Place Prepared

Do you think that the God who has provided so amply for living has made no provision for dying? Bear this in mind: the hope of eternal life rests solely and exclusively upon your faith in Jesus Christ! Make no mistake about that.

Before He told His disciples about the many "mansions" or resting places, and before He gave them the hope of heaven,

Jesus said, "Trust in God; trust also in me." Then He went on to tell them, "I am going there to prepare a place for you," and He gave them the added assurance, "I am the way and the truth and the life. No one comes to the Father except through me" (John 14:1–6).

Eternal life is by and through the Lord Jesus Christ. To put it in the Bible's exact words, here is the secret of the blessed hope: "Whoever believes in the Son has eternal life, but whoever rejects the Son will not see life" (John 3:36).

When a true believer dies, he goes straight into the presence of Christ. He goes to heaven to spend eternity with God. By terrible contrast, the person who rejects God's offer of pardon is separated from God, a place that Jesus called hell.

My wife, Ruth, said it well in a poem she wrote some years ago:

> When death comes
> will it come quietly
> —one might say creep—
> as after a hard
> and tiring day, one lies
> and longs for sleep—
> ending age and sorrow
> or youth and pain?
> Who dies in Christ
> has all to gain
> —and a Tomorrow!
> Why weep?
>
> Death may be savage.
> We cannot be sure:
> the godly may be slaughtered,
> evil men endure;
> however death may strike,
> or whom,
> who knows the risen Lord
> knows, too, the empty tomb.[1]

---

1. Ruth Bell Graham, *Sitting by My Laughing Fire* (Waco: Word Books, 1977), p. 178.

> *Is it not conceivable that there is still another dimension possible, a world in which the question of an ultimate meaning of human suffering would find an answer?*[1]
>
> VIKTOR E. FRANKL

16/

After Armageddon: The Glory Ahead

DEATH IS NOT the end of the story for the Christian, for we are just "pilgrims" passing through this world with its pain and suffering. There is life beyond death! This is the clear-cut promise of the Scriptures. Modern man has an inherent fear of and an insatiable curiosity concerning what lies beyond the grave. But the Christian can know with certainty what awaits on the other side. The apostle Paul stared the specter of death in the face and exulted, "Where, O death, is your victory? Where, O death, is your sting? The sting of death is sin, and the power of sin is the law. But thanks be to God! He gives us the victory through our Lord Jesus Christ" (1 Cor. 15:55–57).

A young man with an incurable disease was reported to have said, "I don't think I would be afraid to die if I knew what to expect after death." Evidently this young man had not heard of the heaven God has prepared for those who love Him. The man had within him the fear of death. And yet for the Christian there need be no fear. Christ has given us hope. Jesus said, "I am going there to prepare a place for you. And if I go . . . I will come back and take you to be with me that you also may be where I am" (John 14:2,3). And that place,

---

1. Viktor E. Frankl, *Man's Search for Meaning* (Boston: Beacon Press, 1962), p. 120.

according to Paul, is vastly better than anything on earth. He wrote, "I desire to depart and be with Christ, which is better by far" (Phil. 1:23).

For the Christian, the grave is not the end, nor is death a calamity, for he has a glorious hope—the hope of heaven. We are assured of our entrance into heaven at the moment we commit our lives to Christ.

Heaven has been depicted in many ways in books and films. However, the Bible gives us a glimpse of its glory which no fiction writer could imagine.

Heaven Is a Home

First, heaven is home. The Bible takes the word *home* with all of its tender associations and sacred memories, and applies it to the hereafter and tells us that heaven is home.

Just before Christ went to the cross, He gathered His disciples in the upper room and talked about a home. He said, "In my Father's house are many rooms" (John 14:2). When Jesus spoke of heaven as "my Father's house," He was referring to it as home. The Father's house is always His children's home. Paul spoke of believers who have departed this life as being "at home with the Lord" (2 Cor. 5:8).

Second, heaven is a home which is permanent. One of the unfortunate facts about the houses which men build for themselves is that they are not permanent. Houses do not last forever. It is true of the house, the outer shell, and it is true of the family. How quickly the children grow up and leave home.

Wonderful as our homes and families may be, they are not permanent. Sometimes I look at my own children and can hardly believe they are all grown and on their own—and have made me a grandfather many times over. My wife and I are alone in an empty house that once rang with the laughter of five children.

When Jesus said, "In my Father's house are many mansions" (KJV), we find a very interesting meaning for the word *mansion.* The Greek word used does not mean an imposing house but a resting place. The expression is translated in the margin of the American Standard Version as "abiding places." This comes from the same stem as the English word *remain.*

During Christ's ministry on earth He had no home. He once said, "Foxes have holes and birds of the air have nests, but the Son of Man has no place to lay his head" (Matt. 8:20).

His home in heaven is not transitory, however, but permanent.

The early disciples who for Christ's sake had given up houses and lands and loved ones knew little of home life or home joys. Christian pilgrims suffer in many ways, and Jesus knew it—for He suffered more severely than any of His followers. It was as if Jesus had said to them: "We have no lasting home here on earth, but my Father's house is a home where we will be together for all eternity."

Amid all the changes which sooner or later will come to break up the earthly home, we have the promise of a home where Christ's followers will remain forever. Paul said at one time, "So we will be with the Lord forever" (1 Thess. 4:17). Our permanent home is not here on earth. Our permanent home is heaven.

Sometimes when things do not go right down here, we grow homesick for heaven. Many times in the midst of the sin, suffering, and sorrow of this life there is a tug at our soul. That is homesickness coupled with anticipation.

Some believers are lying on hospital beds today, some are in mental institutions, some are suffering from terrible diseases or financial loss or bereavement, in prisons, labor camps, or held as hostages. They are weary of earth, with all its troubles and toils, and are longing for home. The home that awaits them is heaven.

Third, the Bible teaches that heaven is a home which is beautiful. Almost everyone likes to beautify his home. There is something lacking in a home where there are no flowers, no pictures on the walls, where no effort at all has been put forth to make the home attractive.

Few of us here have homes as beautiful as we would like, but everyone in heaven will find it beautiful beyond imagination. Heaven could not help but be so, because it is the Father's house and He is a God of beauty.

Look at the world around us. God made it! Whether we live amid the snow and ice of Alaska or under the palm trees of California or Florida, we have beauty. I have traveled all over

America and in many parts of the world. I have never seen a place that I did not think had some charm and beauty, except where man has spoiled it.

There is even something about a bleak desert or a bare mountaintop that has its charm. It seems that all of nature is beautiful and only man's work is ugly.

Nothing made by the hand of man has ever been so beautiful as starlight on the water or moonlight on the snow. And the same hand that made trees and fields and flowers, the seas and hills, the clouds and sky, has been making a home for us called heaven.

It is a place so beautiful that when the apostle John caught a glimpse of it, the only thing to which he could liken it was a young woman at the crowning moment of her life: her wedding day. He said that the holy city was like "a bride beautifully dressed for her husband" (Rev. 21:2).

Fourth, the Bible teaches that heaven will be a home which is happy. I know many beautiful homes that are unhappy. They are homes made beautiful by everything that culture and wealth can provide, yet there is something lacking. These homes bring to mind the wise man's words, "Better a dry crust with peace and quiet than a house full of feasting, with strife" (Prov. 17:1).

God's house will be a happy home because there will be nothing in it to hinder happiness (Rev. 21:4). This world has in it much happiness for those who know how to find it—but it is basically an unhappy planet where suffering and pain prevail.

Think of a place where there will be no sin, no sorrow, no quarrels, no misunderstandings, no hurt feelings, no pain, no sickness, no suffering, no death.

The Father's house will be happy because it is a place of music and song. We sing when we are happy. In heaven everyone is singing. Its inhabitants sing "a new song," ascribing glory to Him who was slain and who ransomed men to God by His blood (Rev. 5:9). Again, later on we hear the voice of a great multitude, like the sound of many waters, crying, "Hallelujah! For our Lord God Almighty reigns" (19:6). It sounds as though heaven is one long Hallelujah Chorus!

The Father's house will be a happy home because there will also be work to do. Certainly this is true in every well-ordered home on earth. But it will be the kind of work we have never experienced on earth. We will labor without failure, frustration, or fatigue.

Revelation 22:3 tells us that in heaven there will be "no curse." This is a reference to God's judgment upon Adam in the Garden of Eden. After the Fall, Adam's work became toilsome and strenuous. No doubt this was a safety precaution on God's part, designed to keep the rebellious Adam out of "mischief." God ordained that his work would require more time and effort, leaving less time to sin.

But in heaven our work will be creative, stimulating, and productive.

In Revelation 22:3, John wrote, "His servants will serve him." Each one will be given the task that fits his powers, his tastes and his talents. Perhaps God will give us new worlds to conquer. Perhaps He will send us to explore some distant planet or star, there to proclaim His message of everlasting love. Whatever we do, or wherever we go, the Bible says we will serve Him.

Think of working forever at something you love to do, for one you love with all your heart, and never getting tired! We will never know weariness in heaven.

And the Father's house will be a happy home because friends will be there. Have you ever been to a strange place and had the joy of seeing a familiar face? Not one of us who enters the Father's house will feel lonely or strange, for our friends will be there.

Many people write me and ask, "Will we know each other in heaven?" Certainly we will know each other in heaven. On the Mount of Transfiguration, did not Elijah and Moses know each other? And in the story that Jesus told about the rich man and Lazarus, did not the rich man after death recognize Lazarus and Abraham?

If you are a believer, you are going to see again those who have accepted Christ. In heaven families and friends will be reunited.

God's house will be a happy home because Christ will be there. He will be the center of heaven. To Him all hearts will turn and upon Him all eyes will rest.

What is going to make heaven so delightful? It won't be the pearly gates; it won't be the jasper walls; it will be that we shall behold the King in His beauty and see Him face to face.

In Revelation 22 we are told that we "will see his face" (v.4). Our relationship with Christ will be an intimate one. Have you ever stood in the midst of a crowd at a parade or convention and strained to see an important dignitary? Or have you attended a retreat or conference and wished that somehow the main speaker might take special notice of you? Although there will be millions of Christians in heaven, we won't have to settle for a passing glimpse of the one we love. Jesus will know each of us personally, and we shall know Him in a deeper way than ever before. "Now we see but a poor reflection; then we shall see face to face. Now I know in part; then I shall know fully, even as I am fully known" (1 Cor. 13:12).

The Bible also tells us that heaven will be a happy home because we will be immune from suffering.

Martin Luther King during the civil rights movement used to exclaim that he looked forward to heaven where he would be "Free at last." That is the inscription on his tomb in Atlanta.

In Revelation 7:17 and 21:4 John writes: "For the Lamb at the center of the throne will be their shepherd; he will lead them to springs of living water. And God will wipe away every tear from their eyes. . . . There will be no more death or mourning or crying or pain, for the old order of things has passed away." When we get to heaven, all our suffering will be over.

We will also be immune from the sin which brought the suffering upon us to begin with. We who have been troubled and tempted by sin in our pilgrimage through this world will no longer be affected by this Satan-inspired problem. Our enemy will be cast into hell, to be eternally separated from God and His people. Because Jesus conquered Satan once for all on the cross, we will live in an environment in which sin will be permanently defeated in our lives.

Heaven—a Place of Immortality

God has promised us new bodies for our new home. Heaven will be a place of immortality.

Paul told the Corinthians, "For the perishable must clothe itself with the imperishable, and the mortal with immortality.

When the perishable has been clothed with the imperishable, and the mortal with immortality, then the saying that is written will come true: 'Death has been swallowed up in victory'" (1 Cor. 15:53,54).

What this means is that once we have reached heaven, we will no longer be troubled or inhibited by physical or bodily limitations. Can you imagine that? The crippled, diseased, wasted bodies will be strong and beautiful and vigorous.

Once there was a widow and her son who lived in a miserable attic. Years before, she had married against her parents' wishes and had gone with her husband to live in a foreign land.

He had proved irresponsible and unfaithful, and after a few years he died without having made any provision for her and the child. It was with the utmost difficulty that she managed to scrape together the bare necessities of life.

The happiest times in the child's life were those when the mother took him in her arms and told him about her father's house in the old country. She told him of the grassy lawn, the noble trees, the wild flowers, the lovely pictures, and the delicious meals.

The child had never seen his grandfather's home, but to him it was the most beautiful place in all the world. He longed for the time when he would go there to live.

One day the postman knocked at the attic door. The mother recognized the handwriting on the letter he brought and with trembling fingers broke the seal. There was a check and a slip of paper with just two words: "Come home."

Some day a similar experience will be ours—an experience shared by all who know Christ. We do not know when the call will come. It may be when we are in the midst of our work. It may be after weeks or months of illness. But some day a loving Hand will be laid upon our shoulder and this brief message will be given: "Come home."

All of us who know Christ personally need not be afraid to die. Death to the Christian is "going home."

Heaven—a Holy City

The Book of Revelation pictures heaven as a city, the new Jerusalem—a perfect environment in which a perfect society dwells.

> Then I saw a new heaven and a new earth, for the first heaven and the first earth had passed away, and there was no longer any sea. I saw the Holy City, the new Jerusalem, coming down out of heaven from God, prepared as a bride beautifully dressed for her husband (Rev. 21:1,2).

The characteristics of the new Jerusalem are described in chapters 21 and 22. They reveal that heaven will be a place whose inhabitants will be free from the fears and insecurities which plague and haunt us in our present lives.

In heaven there will be no fear of an energy crisis. Heaven's natural resources will never be depleted. And there will be no competition over the distribution of those resources. We are told that on "main street" of the new Jerusalem the tree of life will be situated. All nations will have access to it. John describes it as "the tree of life, bearing twelve crops of fruit, yielding its fruit every month. And the leaves of the tree are for the healing of the nations" (22:2). Harmony will reign among heaven's population, and there will be no fear of political unrest and upheavals.

The inhabitants of the city will be free from the economic and financial pressures that burden us here on earth. Many of you are struggling to support your families. You won't need to worry about taking a second job in order to feed your family when you get to heaven. The Bible tells us that God will invite us to "drink without cost from the spring of the water of life" (21:6). We will not have to work in order to survive. We will be active, to be sure. But we will work for the sheer joy of creating and producing. In a sense, our work will be our recreation.

In heaven we will be free from the fear of personal physical harm. Several features indicate this. There will be no night (22:5). Evil lurks when darkness falls upon a city. The majority of our crimes occur after sunset. But in the new Jerusalem there will be no night in which arsonists, robbers, and rapists might prowl. In fact, there will be no evil people in heaven to frighten and hurt us (21:8,27).

And the gates of this city will never close (21:25). Ancient cities were fortified by means of high walls and gates which would be closed and locked at night, thus protecting their inhabitants from roving bands of robbers and enemies. There will be no one to fear in the heavenly city, so the gates will remain open. We will be able to travel in and out of the city with complete security. We must remember that ancient cities depended upon natural lighting, the sun and moon, for their source of illumination. But in the new Jerusalem, God's glory will illumine every street and alley. We will be able to walk in the peace and security of His presence.

One of man's greatest insecurities is his fear of personal failure. Sometimes in our various employments, responsibilities, relationships, and activities there are obstacles to our success. For one reason or another, we fail. We are smitten with guilt, shame, and a deeper sense of insecurity. But in heaven we will know no failure. We will succeed in what we undertake, for there shall be "no curse" (22:3). As we pointed out earlier, God's judgment upon man will be lifted. Our work will be free of frustration, and there will be no sense of failure. Our work will be invigorating and inspiring.

Spiritually, there will be no fear of separation or feelings of distance from God. Our relationship with Him will be intimate and direct. There will be no temple in the new Jerusalem (21:22). Ancient cities were filled with temples, buildings in which men attempted to reach out to God. In heaven there will be no need for a temple, for God's people will live in His presence and praise Him continually. There will be no "dry periods" in our spiritual existence, for we shall live in unbroken communion with the Lord.

Have you ever wondered how much better you might have done in school if you had really applied yourself? Do you sometimes feel that if you had been better disciplined in your training you would have made the varsity sports team? What would it be like if you could be consistent in the exercise of godly virtues such as patience, gentleness, and self-control? What latent talents and abilities do you possess which could be of benefit to yourself and others?

I think that when we reach heaven, we will have our potentials fully realized. We will know the kind of people we can really be when God is allowed to have full control of our lives. Revelation describes the heavenly inhabitants, the new society, as gems radiating their beauty in the presence of a great light. It speaks of "the Holy City, Jerusalem, coming down out of heaven from God. It shone with the glory of God, and its brilliance was like that of a very precious jewel, like a jasper, clear as crystal" (21:10,11).

When a newly engaged young lady shows off her diamond ring, she will often escort her audience to a window or lamp. The features of the gem are best seen as it reflects the light. This might well express how God will bring out the best in each one of us. There will be no sin to mar the beauty of His people, and we will reflect His glory.

According to the Bible, heaven is a strong city in which we shall dwell securely, released from the fears that oppress us. We will be free to become the whole, productive, and happy people God intends us to be.

Heaven—a Glorious Garden

Revelation also pictures heaven as being a garden, where the tree of life and river of life will abundantly refresh its inhabitants. God will walk with His people in perfect fellowship. In Genesis we read that man's perfect environment was destroyed. In Revelation we read that the Garden of Eden will be restored.

To the penitent thief on the cross Jesus said, "Today you will be with me in paradise" (Luke 23:43). *Paradise* is derived from a Persian word meaning a garden. Jesus was promising the thief a place in the garden of God.

Here is another beautiful picture of what heaven is like. As Isaac Watts put it in one of his hymns, "There everlasting spring abides, And never-withering flowers." In that delightful environment we shall dwell with Christ in perfect harmony and happiness.

Heaven—a Beautiful Bride

The heavenly society is also pictured as a bride arrayed for her wedding day (21:2,9). Why does God call His people a bride? This is a particularly precious and meaningful description of our relationship to God and the responsibilities associated with it.

1. A bride is an object of her husband's love. In Eastern culture (the culture in which Revelation was written), weddings are often arranged years in advance of the actual event. This is a picture of God's love for us. In 1 John 4:19 we read, "We love [God] because *he first loved us*" (italics mine). In Ephesians we are told that God's love for us extends back even before the beginning of time. This tells us that we are special to God, that we are valuable to Him, that in His eyes we have real worth. Do you realize that God loves *you?*

A bride is brought into a loving relationship with her husband. The engagement has secured the relationship. It is through Christ that our relationship with God is established.

Have you invited Christ into your life and established a permanent relationship with God? Are you certain of your future home? Do you know without a doubt that the glory ahead is assured for you?

The Bible tells us that heaven will usher us into a new experience with God, just like a bride embarking on a new life with her husband. The Christian life is a most exciting life. And heaven will unfold totally new adventures for us.

2. A bride prepares herself for her wedding day. Have you ever seen a bride walk down the aisle in a dirty wedding gown? Rarely! God gives us the responsibility of preparing ourselves to live with Christ in heaven, that we may be presented to the Bridegroom "holy and blameless" (Eph. 5:27). The apostle Peter, in writing about the new heaven and earth coming, exhorted his readers: "So then, dear friends, since you are looking forward to this, *make every effort* to be found spotless, blameless and at peace with him [the Lord]" (2 Pet. 3:14, italics mine). "You ought to live holy and godly lives as you look forward to the day of God and speed its coming" (vv.11,12).

3. A bride invites her friends to her wedding. God wants us to invite others to the great wedding feast that He is preparing. All around you are people who do not know Christ—friends, neighbors, business associates, family members. They have no hope of heaven and no assurance of God's presence and help in this life. Are you praying for them? Are you seeking to share Christ with them? Are you a witness to the reality of God's love and power in your own life?

Remember, the task of evangelism is not just the job of a few people who are called by God to be evangelists or pastors—it is the privilege and responsibility of every believer. Paul said concerning the Thessalonian Christians, "The Lord's message rang out from you not only in Macedonia and Achaia—your faith in God has become known everywhere" (1 Thess. 1:8). May this be true of each one of us, as we invite others to come to Christ by faith.

I believe we are living in the most challenging generation in history. As the world rushes headlong toward Armageddon, our attention should be centered on telling everyone about the One who is waiting to give us relief from this suffering world.

In the Bible God gives us a glimpse of what heaven will be like for the believer. It will have the characteristics of a happy home, a holy city, a glorious garden, and a beautiful bride. This staggers the imagination!

God has prepared a place that will give us relief from suffering and renewed vitality for serving the Savior. As Paul so aptly penned, "I consider that our present sufferings are not worth comparing with the glory that will be revealed in us" (Rom. 8:18).

An unknown devotional writer has said:

> Heaven is a place of complete victory and triumph. *This* is the battlefield; *there* is the triumphal procession. *This* is the land of the sword and spear; *that* is the land of the wreath and crown. Oh, what a thrill of joy shall shoot through the hearts of all the blessed when their conquests shall be complete in heaven, when death itself, the last of foes, shall be slain—when Satan shall be dragged captive at the chariot wheels of Christ—when he shall have overthrown sin—when the great shout of universal victory shall rise from the hearts of all the redeemed.

Yes, in the present world we are in the midst of a battlefield. We often experience (with Paul) what it means to be "harassed at every turn—conflicts on the outside, fears within" (2 Cor. 7:5). But God is with us if we have committed our lives to Christ. Christ has made us His own, and nothing "will be able to separate us from the love of God that is in Christ Jesus our Lord" (Rom. 8:39). The Holy Spirit dwells within us, and "the

Spirit helps us in our weakness" (Rom. 8:26). And, as we have seen, God is able to sanctify the suffering and adversity we face and use it to draw us closer to Himself and mold us into the people He wants us to be.

But ahead of us is the triumphal procession—the glorious victory and reality of heaven. Some day we will see "a new heaven and a new earth, the home of righteousness" (2 Pet. 3:13). Some day "the trumpet will sound, the dead will be raised imperishable, and we will be changed" (1 Cor. 15:52). Some day we will receive "an inheritance that can never perish, spoil or fade—kept in heaven for you" (1 Pet. 1:4). Some day "when he appears, we shall be like him, for we shall see him as he is" (1 John 3:2). Some day the suffering and pain of this world will be over, and we will be with God forever in heaven.

Until that glorious day—"Till Armageddon"—let us live for Christ. Let us trust Him. Let us turn to Him in our time of need. And let us joyfully walk hand in hand with our Lord Jesus Christ—regardless of our circumstances—until we personally and physically join Him throughout eternity!

> *I consider that our present sufferings are not worth comparing with the glory that will be revealed in us.*
> ROMANS 8:18

Scripture Index